A SENSE OF PLACE
Re-Evaluating Regionalism in Canadian and American Writing

*Re-Evaluating Regionalism in
         Canadian and American Writing*

A Sense of Place

*Edited by Christian Riegel, Herb Wyile,
Karen Overbye and Don Perkins*

The University of   *Textual Studies in Canada* 9
Alberta Press   Spring 1997

Published by
   The University of Alberta Press
   Ring House 2
   Edmonton, Alberta, Canada   T6G 2E1
      and
   Textual Studies in Canada
   Faculty of Arts
   Box 3010
   The University College of the Cariboo
   Kamloops, British Columbia   V2C 5N3

© The University of Alberta Press 1998

Notice to librarians: *A Sense of Place*, a special issue co-published in book form with the University of Alberta Press, is *Textual Studies in Canada* 9, Spring 1997, ISSN 1183-854X.

General editors for the series: W.F. Garrett-Petts, Henry Hubert, James Hoffman, and Katherine Sutherland
Manuscript editors: W.F. Garrett-Petts and Henry Hubert
Copyeditors: James Hoffman and Katherine Sutherland
Text formatting: Dennis Keusch
Book design: Alan Brownoff

All rights reserved.
No part of this publication may be produced, stored in a retrieval system, or transmitted in any forms or by any means, electronic, mechanical, photocopying, recording, or otherwise, without the prior permission of the copyright owner.

Printed on acid-free paper.
First edition, second printing, 2006
Printed and bound by Blitzprint, Calgary, Alberta, Canada.

The University of Alberta Press acknowledges the financial support of the Government of Canada through the Book Publishing Industry Development Program for our publishing activities. The Press also gratefully acknowledges the support received for its program from the Canada Council for the Arts and the Alberta Foundation for the Arts.

Canadian Cataloguing in Publication Data

Main entry under title:
A sense of place

   Papers from a conference held in Edmonton, Oct. 13–15, 1995.
   Includes bibliographical references and index.
   ISBN 10: 0-88864-310-1
   ISBN 13: 978-0-88864-310-0

Copublished by: Textual Studies in Canada.
   1. Regionalism in literature—Congresses. 2. Canadian literature—History and criticism—Congresses. 3. American literature—History and criticism—Congresses. 4. Literature, Comparative—Canadian and American. 5. Literature, Comparative—American and Canadian. I. Riegel, Christian Erich, 1968– II. Wyile, Herb, 1961–
PS8101.R36S46 1997   C810.9'971
                       C97-911026-2
PR9185.5.R36S46 1997

Canadian Cataloguing in Publication Data

Textual Studies in Canada

   1. Canadian literature and language—Criticism and interpretation—Theory.
   2. Rhetoric and composition. 3. Discourse analysis.
   I. Title. II. Series: Textual Studies in Canada.

Contents

Acknowledgements VII

Introduction: Regionalism Revisited IX
HERB WYILE, CHRISTIAN RIEGEL,
KAREN OVERBYE, DON PERKINS

Toward the Ends of Regionalism 1
FRANK DAVEY

Writing Out of the Gap: Regionalism, Resistance,
and Relational Reading 19
MARJORIE PRYSE

"Regionalist" Fiction and the Problem of Cultural Knowledge 35
DAVID MARTIN

Reassessing Prairie Realism 51
ALISON CALDER

West of "Woman," Or, Where No Man Has Gone Before: Geofeminism
in Aritha Van Herk 61
W.M. VERHOEVEN

Is Newfoundland Inside that T.V.?: Regionalism, Postmodernism, and
Wayne Johnston's *Human Amusements* 81
JEANETTE LYNES

Magic Environmentalism: Writing/Logging (in) British Columbia   95
RICHARD PICKARD

Afterword: Sense of Place: A Response to Regionalism   113
JONATHAN HART

Bibliography   119

Index   127

Acknowledgements

THE EDITORS WOULD LIKE TO ACKNOWLEDGE a publication grant awarded through the Office of the Vice President Research, Ron Kratochvil, at the University of Alberta. We would also like to thank the sponsorship of the Department of English at the University of Alberta, and its chairs, during the planning and execution of the Sense of Place Conference, Shirley Neuman and Patricia Demers, the sponsorship of the University of Alberta Graduate Students Association, the University of Alberta Conference Fund, the Dean of Arts, Patricia Clements, and the Canada Council. Astrid Blodgett, Leslie Loshack-Kiist, Mary Marshall-Durrell, and June McLellan of the English Department, deserve particular mention for their assistance with administrative matters. We would also like to thank Dan Coleman for generously sharing his knowledge of conference planning and publishing.

From its inception, this book has been a collaborative effort with the editors of *Textual Studies in Canada*, who supervised the refereeing and selection of the articles and coordinated the copublication with the University of Alberta Press. Our thanks go to the editors, W.F. Garrett-Petts, Henry Hubert, James Hoffman and Katherine Sutherland, as well as their Editorial Advisory Board and Dennis Keusch. Their enthusiastic response to our initial proposal, their insightful reading of and commentary on the various permutations of the manuscript, and their commitment to bringing this project to fruition are greatly appreciated. An acknowledgement here doesn't do justice to the truly collaborative nature of the process, or to the goodwill of the editors of *Textual Studies in Canada* in dealing with the challenges of communicating effectively across great distances to ultimately see this book through to its final stages.

This special issue is copublished in book form with the University of Alberta Press. In preparing the copublication, the expertise of Glenn

Rollans, Alan Brownoff, Leslie Vermeer and Mary Mahoney-Robson at the University of Alberta Press is also acknowledged.

Finally, the editors would like to thank Mary Chapman for her support of the project.

HERB WYILE, CHRISTIAN RIEGEL,
KAREN OVERBYE, DON PERKINS   *University of Alberta*

Introduction

Regionalism Revisited

FOR MOST NORTH AMERICANS, identity is a complex mix of a feeling of community, a shared cultural, ethnic and social background, and an attachment to place—a mix that is much more localized than the feeling of being Canadian or being American. In *The Betweenness of Place: Towards a Geography of Modernity*, Nicholas Entrikin argues for the centrality of place in the construction of subjectivity in contemporary society: "Place presents itself to us as a condition of human experience. As agents in the world we are always 'in place,' much as we are always 'in culture.' For this reason our relations to place and culture become elements in the construction of our individual and collective identities" (1). Regionalism, as a prevalent term in public and institutional discourses in North America, has played a significant role in giving expression to that sense of identification, though attitudes towards regionalism in those discourses have been at best ambivalent. However, current global trends are investing the term with new significance, necessitating a new look at the way the term has been and can be used to examine social, cultural and political relationships.

Despite its prevalence in public and academic commentary and the often charged and emotive connotations of the term, regionalism lacks clear definition. As Benedict Anderson argues, the idea of nationalism by the late twentieth century has become entirely naturalized and it is assumed that "in the modern world everyone can, should, will 'have' a nationality, as he or she 'has' a gender" (13); regionalism, in a similar fashion, has come to be accepted as a discourse or form of identification or (following Benedict Anderson's view of nationalism) a kind of kinship—if not viewed as being as significant a component of identity as nationality, then at least not far off.

In Canada, Janine Brodie observes, "[r]eferences to region are so familiar and pervasive that we have accepted these divisions as natural and self-evident without ever questioning why we have come to think of the country in these terms or what meanings these spatial abstractions actually convey" (6). Increasingly, however, critics are viewing region and regionalism as constructs rather than as natural formations and recognizing the processes of negotiation, contestation and conflict in forming their definition. That is, they are exploring and questioning not just what constitutes a particular region (the American Midwest, for instance, or the cross-border Great Plains) or a particular regionalism (such as Maritime regionalism or Southern regionalism), but what *region* and *regionalism* themselves mean.

The image of regionalism, indeed, has been a divided one, especially because regionalism has been largely defined in relation to nationalism, sometimes as a centrifugal, even corrosive force undermining the cohesion of the nation-state, sometimes as a more organic alternative to the nation-state with its arbitrary borders. This tension between views of regionalism is a long-standing one: as Raymond Williams notes in *Keywords*, the etymological roots of the word *region* point to both autonomy (a region as a cohesive entity in its own right) and subordination (a region as part of a larger entity), and the history of the terms *region* and *regionalism* reflects a struggle between these two readings. That such a tension is alive and well is amply illustrated in current global politics, from the former Yugoslavia and Soviet Union to Canada, signifying the importance, and difficulty, of defining region and regionalism.

Noting these shifting views of regionalism is important if we are to understand the situation of the terms as they are deployed in literary criticism and theory. As part of the larger concern with place in literature, particularly in Canada and the United States, region and regionalism have contributed to an important, if not central, paradigm within which to view writers and their work. The term regionalism is used alternately to describe the unifying principle of a corpus of literary texts (that is, a regional literature), the attachment of a writer to a particular place, the diversity of writing within the larger body of a national literature, or a kind of ideological consciousness or discourse. Regional movements and/or the concentration of literary activity in particular regions at particular times have certainly been recognized—such as the New England "Renaissance" in the mid-ninteenth century; the role of regionalism in the development of realism in turn-of-the-century America; the "New Regionalism" between the two world wars, especially in the South; and the flourishing of literary activity on the Canadian Prairies in the 1960s and 70s. Finally, the association of particular writers with their regions has been a central focus in considerations of their work (an association which often carries connotations of possession or authority): Mark Twain's Mississippi, Jack Hodgins's Vancouver Island, William Faulkner's Yoknapatawpha, Robert Frost's New England, Margaret Laurence's Manawaka.

These applications of the concept of regionalism in literary critical practice raise a number of issues, such as the influence of place on a writer's work, the principles according to which one draws regional divisions among writers, and the effect such an association has on the assessment of a writer's work. While similar issues are raised in literary critical considerations of nation, race and gender, the concept of regionalism occupies a much more uneasy place in literary studies. As Michael Kowalewski argues, "[t]he critical assumption seems to be that region or a sense of place is not an imaginative factor that can be internalized and struggled with in the same literarily rewarding ways that writers struggle with issues of race, class, and gender" (174). The use of the term *regionalism*, indeed, has always been a conflicted one, bringing into view tensions between the centre and the periphery, the rural and the urban, the local and the cosmopolitan, the regional and the national. Not only are the boundaries between the different uses of the term in literary criticism not always clear (what, for instance, makes a regional writer?), but the very value of regionalism is a matter of debate (is regionalism, for instance, as some critics would have it, a terminal condition?).

While regionalism in both its cultural and political forms has at times been seen as a positive force, a healthy heterogeneity and difference, or even the very variety out of which a nation, its culture, its literature are constituted, regionalism has been regarded predominantly as suspect, second-rate, even corruptive. In the history of criticism in both Canada and the United States, regionalism has been associated, often unfavourably, with provincialism, with a rural context, or with local-colour writing. Canadian critic E.K. Brown, for instance, argued in 1943 that "the advent of regionalism may be welcomed with reservations as a stage through which it may be well for us to pass, as a discipline and a purgation," one which will delay "the coming of great books" (21).

In response to political, social and cultural currents, particularly the rise and fall of nationalist sentiments, regionalism has moved in and out of the spotlight throughout the twentieth century. During this time, characterized by the intersection of a humanist sensibility—with its emphasis on the universality of experience—and a nationalism focused predominantly on the borders of the nation-state, regionalism "has been relegated to the periphery of North American literature and criticism" (Jordan 78). But in the last twenty years, economic, political and cultural developments have prompted a renewed focus on regionalism. Decentralization, regional consciousness, and a growing suspicion of institutional nationalism, combined with the development of a global economy and a more eclectic international culture, have undermined the cohesion of the nation-state. The rationalizing effects of a global market economy have put pressures on local economies and cultures, throwing increasing attention on culture and politics at the regional level, and forcing a redefinition of the notion of community.

Changing currents of critical theory have also contributed to new attitudes towards regionalism. The deconstructive and anti-totalizing tendencies of post-structuralist thought have contributed a decentralizing approach to literary criticism and literary history, which in Canada and the United States have been dominated by a centralizing nationalism that privileges the cultural capitals of North America: New York, Los Angeles, and Toronto. Critics are increasingly recognizing such nationalist scholarship as a set of discursive strategies underpinned by questionable political, cultural and aesthetic assumptions; they are recognizing in regionalism an alternative and equally legitimate discourse. This resistance is part of a larger critique of cultural hegemony and a recognition and celebration of diversity. Critics interested in regionalism—along with feminist and post-colonial critics—have recognized the homogenizing and decontextualizing effects of the formalist critical principles which have predominated through most of the twentieth century, and have resisted the ostensibly universalizing patterns, motifs, archetypes and structures that have effectively marginalized regional, women's, and post-colonial writing.

Shifting the focus to regionalism, however, is not an unproblematic move, since regionalism as a political and literary discourse is underpinned by assumptions that warrant interrogation; region, like race, gender, class and sexuality, is not an unproblematic category and must be theorized not in isolation but in relation to other elements central to the construction of subjectivity and of literature. Fortunately, critics are starting to appreciate both the need to re-evaluate regionalism in light of changes in the structures of global politics, economics and culture, and to explore regionalism in the context of contemporary critical theory and the pressing concerns of our times. Feminist critics, for instance, are increasingly challenging the masculinist bias underpinning definitions of region and regionalism, highlighting the contribution of women writers to regional literatures all over North America. Contemporary critiques of canonicity and representation also extend to regionalism, for the deconstruction of the principles underlying canonicity and canon formation (and of the notion of writers as representatives) can be applied to writing at the regional level as it has been at the national level. Another important dimension of the contemporary re-evaluation of regionalism is the attempt to theorize cultural difference and ethnicity in relation to regionalism (and vice versa). The relationship between ethnicity and region is an important one, highlighting the complex connections between place, subjectivity, and culture, and pointing to the need to define the writing of particular regions in more pluralistic terms.

Finally, critics are making efforts to define the role of regionalism within postmodern culture. Postmodernism is associated with an international sensibility that has come about partly through technological innovations in transportation and communication and also through the development of a homogenizing global consumer culture dominated by multinational corporations; these innovations, however, have also created a certain cultural and political dislocation and anxiety, which have thrown attention back on local cultures, on the notion of community—attention that may prove beneficial to a focus on regionalism. Postmodernism also suggests a broad cultural shift whose counter-universalizing and decentralizing tendencies potentially favour the local, the particular, and the specific. At the same time, postmodernist poetics involve a greater focus on language and textuality; and regionalism, because of its association with representational poetics, may continue to be marginalized. To that extent, postmodernism establishes the terms of reference within which the resilience of regionalism can be tested, to see what shape it may take within the centralizing and homogenizing pressures of global consumer culture and to see whether it can break out of the traditional stereotype as an aesthetically conservative form.

The following collection of articles, all of which were originally presented, in shorter form, at the 1995 Sense of Place: Re-evaluating Regionalism in Canadian and American Writing Conference, held at the University of Alberta, provides a timely revisitation of regionalism from a variety of critical angles. The collection opens with two theoretical papers, representing contrasting yet complementary perspectives on issues of region and regionalism. Frank Davey argues that region and regionalism should be situated in reference to ideologies—such as the nation-state, colonialism, and globalization—rather than by geographical locators. Marjorie Pryse demonstrates how regionalist writing by women and non-dominant men employs strategies of resistance, challenging the dominant culture and inviting readers to experience and identify with the position of the disenfranchised Other. Focusing more closely on textual issues, David Martin draws on examples of "local color" American fiction from the late nineteenth century to illustrate the conflicted aims and results of the observer narrator's study of regional life, and by doing so draws parallels between the approaches and concerns of regionalist fiction and anthropological work. Alison Calder asks "What is so compelling about prairie realism?" Her answer shows how extant and highly influential theories of "the prairie" and attitudes towards a select body of texts valued as prairie realism rest on assumptions of documentary authenticity that effectively deny the prairie writer access to the imagination. Issues of the possibilities of representation, geography, and feminism form the basis for Wil Verhoeven's study of Aritha Van Herk's discursive practice in her fiction and non-fiction. Jeanette Lynes explores the compatibility of the regional and the postmodern in an examination of Wayne Johnston's *Human Amusements*, and Richard Pickard's essay examines the regionalism of three British Columbia writers in the context of postmodernism and the positioning of region in global monopoly capitalism. As a re-evaluation of regionalism in Canadian and American writing, this collection of essays provides a comparative approach to the issue within a continental framework by looking at a broad range of writers, and by exploring regionalism on both sides of the border in light of the central political, cultural, literary, and theoretical debates of our times.

FRANK DAVEY   *University of Western Ontario*

Toward the Ends of Regionalism

W H A T   I S twentieth-century Canadian regionalism? Historians, economists, and political scientists have attempted in their various disciplinary ways to answer this question, but not many of us in literary studies. Here attention has been almost entirely on specific regionalisms, in effect allowing the concept itself to be taken for granted. To the various articles and books offering studies of prairie fiction, west coast poetry, Maritime fiction, or Western writing have been added anthologies variously titled or subtitled *The Atlantic Anthology, The Prairie Experience, Western Windows, West Coast Seen, Prairie Writers on Writing, An Anthology of Prairie Poetry, The Maritime Experience, A/long Prairie Lines, Maritime Lines,* as if terms like "prairie," "maritime," "west coast" or "Atlantic" themselves signalled unproblematical categories. The few resistances to regionalism that have emerged from these have tended to be conducted on humanist/individualist grounds—like George Amabile's objection that the notion of a "prairie voice" is "conformist and prescriptive" (94)—and have thus offered little toward the studying of regionalism as a social construction. What I want to do here is consider both region and regionalism not as locations but as ideologies. In the process I will try to situate regionalism and its literary manifestations in Canada among some of the institutions and processes that help shape contemporary ideologies—including the nation state, colonialism, and globalization.

Roger Gibbins begins his 1982 study of regionalism in Canada and the United States with the observation that the term means something different in the two national cultures: in Canada it is understood as a kind of geographic sectionalism, he suggests, and is both "lauded and lamented"; in the U.S. it has been usually perceived as an "integrative phenomenon" that can amalgamate sectionalisms and facilitates their interaction with the national culture and economy (4). Janine Brodie begins her 1990 study *The Political Economy of Canadian Regionalism* by pointing out how frequently Canadian social scientists have confused and interchanged the terms region, regionalism, regional differences, and regional disparities, and have especially confused region and regionalism as terms that both reflect some necessary determination of culture by geography and landform. Brodie argues, and I would strongly agree, that both region and regionalism are social creations, the first constituting a territorial definition of geographic space based on a selection of possible differentiating criteria—a territorial definition that can change as national political policies change, and the second constituting an interpretation of social interests that gives geographic location priority over such other possible interests as gender, ethnicity, class, age, sexual orientation, and race.

I begin with the observations of Gibbins and Brodie because it seems to me that in Canadian literature the understandings of regionalism are, firstly, as a form of geographic sectionalism that segments the literature into regional isolations; secondly, as a kind of geographic determinism that renders the characteristics of these isolations inevitable; and, thirdly, as the product of intuitive regional self-recognition, and have formed a substantial part of the mythological ground of literary criticism. These understandings have been reflected in semantic slippages that have gone considerably beyond those Brodie identifies among region, regionalism, and regional disparity. In Canadian literary criticism regionalism has often been virtually equated with place, as if any signs of specific places in a text directly signalled regionalist ideology. Regionalism has been equated with *hinterland*, with suggestions that writing acts done in so-called "hinterland" situations might necessarily be regionalist, and with disregard for the complex intranational and international power relationships that make any hinterland-centre analysis simplistic. It has been tied to mimetic aesthetics, when it might as easily—given the kinds of writing the various regions of Canada have produced—have been linked to romance, satire, parody, or fantasy. It has been placed in binary opposition to transcendence, usually in a context which implies that both transcendence and the opposition itself are non-political.

I begin with Gibbins and Brodie also because of the clear link both scholars make between regionalism and nation-state ideology. Regionalism is a concern or phenomenon of nation states, a potential part of its intranational power negotiations. A phenomenon that can be divisive and/or integrative, regionalism becomes part of a national politics, Brodie suggests, when national policies result in regional economic differentiations that in turn occasion the national deployment of arguments of regional self-interest. I begin with them as well because I see Canadian literary regionalism as inextricable from political and economic factors and, given the literary criticism so far, as in some need of being re-situated in relation to these.

Regionalism and the Nation State

Unlike other formulations of interests, regionalism operates within the nation state as a kind of territorialization—and I use Deleuze and Guattari's term deliberately in order to place their analyses of political ideology in the background of the arguments I am making here. Specifically, regionalism operates as a transformation of geography into a sign that can conceal the presence of ideology. The individual called to by regionalism is invited to hold certain restraining and shaping beliefs not because of political difference, but because such beliefs are perceived as "true" or "natural" to the inhabiting of a specific geography. In turn, geography acts as a metonym for social identification, enabling in Canada the production of Westerners, Maritimers, northerners, or Cape Breton Islanders, as categories that can override other affiliations.

Yet these regionalist identities are also relative constructions. That is, we would not be here discussing Canadian regionalism were there not also a nation-state called Canada. To some extent regionalism responds to and mimics the homogenizing call of the nation-state, a call made to its citizens as a counter to ethnic, religious, and local loyalties that preceded the formation in the seventeenth and eighteenth centuries of the early nation-states. However, regionalism is not merely one of the possible responses to the unifying strategies of the nation-state, but also a differential term that requires a specific other that is larger, encompassing, but similarly geographic in conception. The nation-state has multiple others—other nation-states, internal political formations, and in recent times multinational or "global" affiliations. The region appears to have mainly the nation-state as its other—this appearance, in fact, is part of regionalist ideology. Differences internal to a regionalism—and I will have more to say about these later—are usually effaced and recuperated by it as contributing to itself: hence we have Maritime women, Atlantic labour histories, prairie populism.

While nation-states are clearly as much if not more geographically defined concepts than are regionalisms, geography usually *seems* more important to regionalism than to the nation-state. The nation-state calls to both its citizens and its borders—defending the latter under the metaphors of integrity and engaging the former under metaphors of community. Regionalism appears to have before all else its geography, calling not to citizens but to people who live in that specific geography.

One of the illusions that a regionalism will often, therefore, incorporate is that while the nation-state is an abstract concept, with exchangeable citizenships and shiftable borders, regionalism has a concrete ground in the geography that it invokes as its region. Strong regionalisms develop narratives and figures that imply the geographic inevitability of the cultural manifestations that partly constitute the region, as in Kreisel's positing that the literature of the Canadian west began "with the impact of the landscape on the mind" (173), Kroetsch's arguments in his infamous essay "Fear of Women in Prairie Fiction" that the prairies have encouraged particular kinds of maleness and femaleness (notably he does not say masculinity or femininity), or Frye's arguments that the "garrison" literature of central Canada had begun with immigrants experiencing their journey up the St. Lawrence estuary as resembling the Biblical Jonah's being devoured by a whale. Regionalisms develop the appearance of having "natural" boundaries—an inside and outside—as if these boundaries were beyond culture. Appeals are constructed to the landscape and climate to explain cultural forms and customs. What is often obscured in these various constructions are the politically oppositional aspects of regionalism: that regionalism is cultural rather than geographic, and represents not geography itself but a strategically resistant mapping of geography in which historic and economic factors play large but largely unacknowledged parts.

Far from being a geographical manifestation, a regionalism is a discourse which contains not only narratives and re-written narratives, but also terms and figurations that generate their meanings differentially within it. As a discourse, it represents a general social or political strategy for resisting meanings generated by others in a nation-state, particularly those generated in geographic areas which can be constructed by the regionalism as central or powerful. However, it is important to note that it is usually also a strategy for resisting other meanings generated in its own region—meanings such as nationalism, feminism, class, ethnicity, localisms, or race. The reliance of regionalist ideology on environmental determinism, on a belief that the landscape has—or should have—effects on the personalities and perspectives of its inhabitants, leads to the assumption that these effects should have greater importance to the individual than do other possible grounds of identity. In the most popular versions (and regionalism is always strongest in its most popular versions), landscape makes the west-coast subject easy going or laid-back, and makes a prairie subject transparent and authentic. In a David Adams Richards novel attention to the land can give characters endurance and survival opportunities, and even intuitively appropriate morality. In E.J. Pratt's early poems the Newfoundland tides "run / Within the sluices of men's hearts." "Red is the sea-kelp on the beach," he writes, "Red as the heart's blood, / . . . / and salt as tears" (2). In a nation-state such an ideology would threaten with irrationalisms of earth and blood the unending political negotiations necessary to polity. In a regionalism, however, because this ideology is popularly concealed beneath touristic images of landcape and inarticulately authentic individuals, there appears to be no ideology.

So far I have mainly discussed regionalism as a particular ideological response to the nation-state. But, equally, a regionalism should be perceived as a production of the nation-state and as partly serving the nation-state's interests. In economics, the myth of geographic determinism allows a national government to avoid responsibility for regional economic downturns, and to use the band-aid of equalization payments instead of investigating ways in which national economic practices create regional economic differentiations. In politics, it allows a national government to deter or limit the growth of transregional ideologies, playing regionalism, for example, against native rights, or against feminism. In culture, regionalist geographic determinism has allowed centralizing critics like W.J. Keith to produce regionalisms as being too specific to be mainstream, and to select for national canonicity—usually on humanist or internationalist grounds—only regional artists who can be constructed as exceptions to this regional specificity.

The most visible and recent regionalisms in the Canadian nation state have been Atlantic/Maritime and Prairie. By visible *regionalisms* I mean those most frequently constructed in anthologies and criticism, and most successfully publicized and commodified as regionalisms both outside and within the geographic areas they claim to regionalize. But successful regionalisms are not necessarily visible regionalisms. In literature at the very least, Southern Ontario regionalism has been successful largely by being invisible, by resisting precise territorial definition, and by passing itself as the Canadian nationalism (a passing which other regionalisms may also aspire to), or as an internationalism. Regionalisms can also be internally successful without meeting similar external success. This usually occurs when the regionalism is more a self-production than a production of the nation state. West Coast regionalism has been much more successful internally in constructing and marketing a "west coast" or a "Pacific" than it has been in constructing these as restricted parts of a national consciousness, or in constructing them in literature as special parts of a national canon. In terms of national canonicity, however, British Columbia writers end little worse off than prairie writers. Like prairie writers, the writers of British Columbia who have been accepted even peripherally as parts of national canonicity have done so mostly on transregional terms—modernism (Wilson, Webb, Birney, Blaser), magic realism (Hodgins), postmodernism (Bowering and Hodgins), feminism (Marlatt and Thomas); while the most self-consciously regional—Howard White, Gerry Gilbert, Peter Trower, Barry McKinnon—have remained largely unknown outside B.C.

Anglo-Quebec writers, through the efforts of editors and critics like Linda Leith and Ken Norris, have also succeeded in constructing themselves as quasi-regionalist, but have not yet succeeded in disseminating this construction with much effect nationally. In part, this lack of success would seem due to the nation-state's need for there not to be an Anglo-Quebec regionalism that could affront or outrage Francophone separatists in their continuing attempts to territorialize francophone culture within Quebec's provincial boundaries. The work of Anglo-Quebec writers that circulates easily outside of Quebec—like that of Gail Scott, Neil Bissoondath, or Mordecai Richler—does so on the basis of other affiliations. Moreover, while Anglo-Quebec tries to present itself as a regionalism nationally, i.e., under the sign of its Quebec location, it presents itself as a linguistic community provincially. The Anglo-Quebec attempt at regionalism offers another instruction in the ideological/cultural dimensions of regionalism.

Within Canada Anglophone-Quebec is a geographic subdivision of the linguistic entity Anglophone-Canadian, rather than a subdivision of a territorial entity. The boundaries of the subdivision, Quebec, however, despite francophone attempts at territorialization, remain political before they are geographic. Moreover, Anglophone-Quebec can make no exclusive claims to territory, nor arguments that geography per se has determined its culture, except in the sense that this geography has been the site of a particular social and political history. One might well translate some of these characteristics of Anglo-Quebec into questions about other Canadian regionalisms, for example asking whether Prairie Canadians can make an exclusive claim to territory (Roger Gibbins has argued here that aboriginal peoples have historically stood aside from prairie regionalism), or whether prairie regionalism's boundaries have not also usually been more political than geographic.

Throughout the Canada of the 1990s it is apparent that in the contemporary industrial nation-state regionalism as a strategy operates within a large interplay of power relations. In parts of a nation-state where, because of historic or economic factors, nationalist or linguistic identifications are readily available, these can either negate a potential regionalism or (as in the case of Ontario and in much of Quebec) become virtually identical with it. Here strategies of resistance to, dissent from, or difference with dominant national ideology cannot take the landscape as ground or metonymy because it has already been taken as a ground for identity by national narratives and iconography. In other spatial parts of the nation, however, regionalism, while available as a discourse of dissent or difference, competes with other discourses, like those of feminism, humanism, ethnicity, or race. For example, a northern regionalism has not developed significant power in Canada because it has remained racially a white figuration, and unable to compete with the discourses of race and ethnicity which structure the Inuit and Dene figurations of land and politics.

Regionalism and Colonialism

Regionalisms can share many of the self-constructions of colonies, although in saying this it is important to note one or two large differences. Colonies usually have clearly defined boundaries, ones in which geophysical markers are consistent with political ones, and which enable the colony to imagine itself separate from the colonizing power. Regionalisms, despite their foregrounding of geography, rarely have a concurrency of geophysical and political boundaries. They thus find themselves both within and without the larger society which they experience as oppositional to them.[1]

Moreover, colonies are political formations, in the sense that they are characterized by internal political differentiation, debate, and process. But regionalisms, although they can have political consequences within the nation-state itself, and interact politically with other nationally contending ideologies, are usually not in themselves political, and have arguably had anti-political effects. Regionalisms propose necessary commonalities that are beyond debate. If regionalisms begin to develop internal differentiation and debate, or to develop institutions to accommodate internal debate, they also begin to include other grounds for identity and individual subjectivity than those of geography, and begin to cease to be regionalisms—a process which appears to have had something to do with the quick decline of regionalist political parties like the Western Canada Concept Party in the 1970s, or the Progressive Party in the 1920s and—if I am following Roger Gibbins's recent arguments (1995) correctly—with the impending decline of the Reform Party. (Reform's failure in the 1997 federal election to expand its representation east of Manitoba, but success in retaining and gaining seats in western Canada, would suggest, according to Gibbins's theory, that it has not yet attempted the political party's task of brokering diversity; it has remained regional by remaining beyond or above non-geographic contentions.) A single-issue party, when that issue is perceived as constructed by landscape, is supportable within the region beyond or across politics. When the party becomes political, encompassing and attempting to accommodate diverse views in order to extend its membership to other parts of Canada (muting, in the Reform case, the call for greater Western representation in federal institutions), it loses its regionalist character.

In Canada, regionalisms tend to exist alongside political movements, occasionally interacting with them, and to be non-identical with provincial boundaries which define and organize non-federal political process. Both "Prairie" and "Maritime" regionalisms extend across three provinces; "Atlantic" regionalism competes conceptually with "Maritime"; British Columbia is not synonymous with "West Coast" regionalism; in fact numerous regionalisms compete here—West Coast, Vancouver Island, up-Island, Interior, Okanagan, Cariboo, Kootenay, Northern, Rocky Mountain, with the latter pretty well straddling the Alberta-B.C. boundary. The fluidity of these boundaries was particularly noticeable in the 1993 federal election, when Manning's Alberta-born Reform Party took 46 of the 58 seats in B.C. and Alberta, but only 5 of the 28 seats in Manitoba and Saskatchewan. Again, it should be noted that this characteristic of regionalism—the conflicts between its geographic and political boundaries

—serves the interests of the nation state, enabling it to weaken regionalisms by calling to the regional inhabitant in terms of other ideological affiliations.

In the contemporary Maritime provinces, a major feature of the recent "regionalism" debates among revisionist historians and political journalists has been this understanding that regionalism as an ideology prevents or conceals internal political differentiation and activism. The journal *New Maritimes* in 1981 embarked on a program of making known the internal political conflicts of the Maritime provinces: the efforts of blacks in Nova Scotia and of Micmacs to retrieve their children from residential schools, the labour struggles in fisheries and manufacturing, and the attempts to establish an effective CCF presence. The fact that most of these efforts ended in failure was made secondary in most of the *New Maritimes* accounts to the desire and vision which motivated the efforts. P.A. Buckner's introduction to his 1986 essay collection *Teaching Maritime Studies* argued the need to replace stereotypes or myths of the Maritimes as a place of political patronage, government corruption, and public conservatism with research that could detail such things as regional and class differences and militant labour movements within the three provinces. Buckner later suggested (1988) that the very concept of "Maritimes" was an homogenizing and essentializing label that has obscured historical and local diversity. E.R. Forbes, in his 1989 study *Challenging the Regional Stereotype: Essays on the 20th Century Maritimes*, set out to confront a number of stereotypes including characterizations of Maritime workers as lazy, of businessmen as timid, of its governments as too short-sighted to emphasize education, and of the culture overall as powerless in the face of national and international economics. The 1986-7 Bell lectures of Acadia University, published as *Beyond Anger and Longing*, were characterized by their editor as proposing that older Maritime responses of anger at non-Maritimers and longing for a return to a lost golden age were counter-productive because they did not make people aware of how they can "actively and collectively create their [own] circumstances" (Fleming 12). All of these publications called for a recognition of political differentiation and conflict within the Maritime region, and recognition also of a history of local initiative, small scale entrepreneurship—although as Alex Dick has argued in an unpublished paper, through their acceptance of the term "Maritimes" and their tendency to seek the binary opposites of the laziness and powerless stereotypes, all have also tended to replace one nostalgic mythology with another:

> Though a contention of Maritime revisionism is the diversity of the region, isolated community action is still used to exemplify a general picture of the "Maritimes." It is then used to advocate an association between the region as a whole and certain eternal verities which the region is supposed to hold, derived by the historian from the historical data. Thus the regional significance of small community action is exaggerated by appeals to mysterious influences for which that community, in its isolated struggle, cannot account. Other [revisionist historians] concede the failure of the independent force of the community in the face of more impressive discourse and systems. Either way, the subject—the people of the Maritimes—is rendered powerless. (8-9)

A literary parallel to these historical and cultural studies is Gwen Davies's essay anthology *Myth and Milieu: Atlantic Literature and Culture*, with its irreverent re-examinations of the work of Helen Creighton, Lucy Maud Montgomery, and Frank Parker Day.

Recent historical writing and cultural writing about Western and Prairie regionalism have reflected some similar interest in replacing mythologies with political, economic, historical, and ideological differentiation. Roger Gibbins's studies have presented prairie regionalism as a social and political phenomenon, as a kind of strategic territorialization within a nation state which has accompanied a perceived sense of the powerlessness of the prairie provinces in national politics. George Melnyk has emphasized historical differentiation within prairie regionalism—a fur trade regionalism succeeded by agrarian and post-agrarian regionalisms, although interestingly, at the end of his *Beyond Alienation: Political Essays on the West*, he calls for the establishment of yet another collective western identity: one of "revolution" and "new beginning" (121). In literature there has been some movement away from regionalist understandings like "west" or "prairies" toward political ones based on provincial boundaries—particularly in anthologies like Fred Stenson's *Alberta Bound*, Robert Kroetsch's *Sundogs: Stories from Saskatchewan*, Geoffrey Ursell's *Saskatchewan Gold*, or Joan Parr's *Manitoba Stories*. Wayne Tefs's introduction to his short story anthology *Made in Manitoba* contains no reference to prairie regionality or to any commonality among the contributors: his references are instead to "gender, geography [that is, the internally differentiating geography of

Manitoba], ethnicity, type, author's wishes, permission fees." In other anthologies, however, like Dennis Cooley's *Inscriptions: A Prairie Poetry Anthology*, Daniel Lenoski's *A/long Prairie Lines: An Anthology of Long Prairie Poems*, and Birk Sproxton's *Trace: Prairie Writers on Writing*, regionalist constructions have persisted. Even here, however, there are fractures. For example, numerous contributors to *Trace* implicitly resist the priority the anthology gives to the "prairie" category—by foregrounding in their essays other categories like gender or ethnicity.

The major characteristic that regionalisms share with colonies is the sense that power over them resides and is wielded elsewhere. In all the large Canadian regionalisms can be found strong resentments toward what the regionalist advocates perceive as the oppositional other, whether this be the Atlantic belief that "Ottawa" has mismanaged Atlantic fishstocks, a Maritime belief that strangers have taken over Maritime cities and their commercial institutions, a prairie resentment that federal elections are decided before the polls close in Manitoba, or a West Coast conviction that Francophone Quebecers recurrently control the national political agenda. A related phenomenon that links regionalisms and colonies is a sense of being unable to change where power resides. For regionalisms, this inability is related to a belief in the region's separation from political process. In the case of the Prairies, of course, the region did begin its existence under the 1870 Manitoba Act and the Crow's Nest Pass Agreement of 1897 as a colony, in the sense that these ensured the region would be a non-industrialized producer of staples and consumer of manufactured goods for Ontario, which was being rapidly industrialized under the shelter of the tariffs of Macdonald's National Policy. The latter policy, together with the building of a national railway network, after 1890 also transformed the Maritime provinces into economic colonies of Quebec and Ontario by its attracting of Maritime bank headquarters and industries to Ontario and Quebec cities that, because of their relative proximity to the new West, were beginning to develop commercial and industrial concentrations.

A third characteristic Canadian regionalisms share with colonialisms is a desire for indigenous or originary grounding of the regionalist ideology. This desire corresponds to the second stage of Frantz Fanon's theory of the evolution of the literatures of colonized peoples, and can be preceded by Fanon's first stage of derivativeness and apprenticeship. The tension between these stages can be seen in Dennis Cooley's *The Vernacular Muse*, where Cooley attempts to totalize much prairie poetry as derivative of British modernism (Fanon's stage one) and to favourably contrast against that an oral poetry that was indigenous by being colloquial, "resistant," "joyous," "subversive," "immediate," "anecdotal," and often marked by verbal excess and ungrammaticality (Fanon's stage two). In prairie literature elsewhere it is manifest in the appeals to the primeval landscape like those made in Mitchell's *Who Has Seen the Wind* and Wiebe's *The Temptations of Big Bear*, or to aboriginal subjects whom white settlers can emulate or even become, like the characters in Newlove's "The Pride" or Laurence's *The Diviners*. (Again such developments serve the interests of the nation-state and national canonicity by allowing the construction of the regionalist culture as atavist and nostalgic.) Fanon's third stage of a "fighting literature," out of movements toward democracy and a diversity of subject positions, is, I suggest, impossible within an ideology of regionalism because once such a political engagement is achieved, individuals will no longer be constructing themselves as preponderantly regional subjects. While Melnyk's call for "revolution" resembles rhetorically Fanon's call for a "fighting literature," there is very little recognition in Melnyk of the ideological diversity in Alberta, Manitoba and Saskatchewan—a diversity that includes feminist, lesbian feminist, aboriginal, urban/rural, ethnic, and class differentiations and cross-differentiations—that any western "revolution" would have to engage and focus.

Regionalism and the Global Economy

For a regionalism to prosper and persist within a contemporary capitalist nation-state some commodification of that regionalism must occur. This commodification could be gastronomic, as in the case of France's Provencal, Breton, and Basque regions, geographic and touristic as in the case of "Supernatural British Columbia," or mytho-cultural, as in the case of Anne of Green Gables. This commodification usually represents a solidifying of Fanon's second stage: the colonial attempt to recover indigenous images and practices. Ideally there are not only products to trade—cod flippers, sockeye salmon, perogies, buffalo meat—but also foundational narratives and images that can be told and sold. But without a certain level of infrastructional development within the communities that share a regionalism, it is difficult for the inhabitants of a regionalism to participate in a commodity-success—and the commodification of the regionalism may serve only to enrich national cultural industries and to prop up national canonicity. Much as large parts of the Atlantic fisheries, the Alberta oil patch, and the B.C. forests have become owned and developed by multinational corporations, simply because the capital for developing these resources has been available mostly elsewhere, many of the narratives and images of a regionalism have been commodified and marketed by individuals and institutions who have at best a tenuous relationship with the regionalism. I am thinking here of how Pratt's early images of Newfoundland fishermen with saltwater in their blood became part of his general standing as a Canadian poet, professor at Victoria College, and author of such national and multinational texts as *The Roosevelt and the Antinoe*, *The Titanic*, and *Behind the Log*, or of how Sinclair Ross's *As For Me and My House* has become the nationally canonical prairie novel through being published in 1941 by a New York publisher (with all its specifically Canadian signs suppressed) and, because it was out of print and cheaply available to the New Canadian Library series, re-published in 1957 by McClelland and Stewart (see Lecker 173-4).

While to some extent the commodification of regionalism that gained strength in the 1970s, particularly in the western provinces, may have seemed to have been a product of the foundation of the Canada Council and its efforts to include criteria of regional equity in its grants to magazine and book publishers, it was at least as much a result of the provincialization of regional economies during this period. The 1970s saw not only the waning of the economic power of the Canadian nation-state, as several provinces began replacing their east-west Canadian ties with north-south continentalist ones, but also a waning of prairie regionalism per se, as Alberta, Saskatchewan, and Manitoba, along with Quebec, embarked on provincial economic policies separate from each other and from those of the nation-state. These new initiatives involved more complex class structures than had the old agrarian independent-farmer economy—capitalist investors, skilled urban workers, a professional class of engineers, economists, and technicians. They were accompanied by a sense of cultural self-consciousness often seen in colonies about to become nations—a self-consciousness that looked to history and mythology as a ground for the attempts at new economic identities—and by the building of cultural infrastructure: arts councils, theatres, publishing houses. Much of the cultural production, however, as I noted in a 1988 essay on "prairie" poetry (*Read-*

ing Canadian Reading 213-30), was nostalgic: poems, novels, and plays that ignored urbanization and the new class complexity, and that attempted to recover the lost nineteenth century lives of settlers and native peoples.

In some genres, like popular history, tourist writing, and pictorial history, there were numerous small-scale attempts to commodify and industrialize old regionalisms. One sees this most clearly in British Columbia and Newfoundland, in photographic books on local scenery, geography, and history—shipwrecks, sealing adventures, ghost-towns— that have for the last three decades been locally produced and sold within tourist industries.

This commodification allowed the reterritorializing of regionalisms as marketplaces, inside which a journal like *New Maritimes* or publishers like Oolichan, Douglas & McIntyre, Thistledown, Western Producer Prairie Books, Acadiensis, or Breakwater could construct readerships, and even begin internal political interrogations. A book like Tefs's *Made in Manitoba*, with a blue band foregrounding the word *Manitoba*, is explicitly directed to Manitoba readers, despite the small print of "22 Great Canadian Stories" above. This commodification often didn't mean that the press published only books of regional interest, but that a plurality of its titles, and often its better-selling ones, foregrounded regional signs. Oolichan's 1994 catalog included, for example, among seven new releases, a book on Parksville, a town on Vancouver Island, one on west coast transportation patterns, and a poetry collection titled *Love in Alaska*. From its backlist the press offered *Salmon Canneries: British Columbia's North Coast, Trout Tales and Salmon Stories, Aboriginal Title in British Columbia,* two books on the history of Vancouver Island coal mining, a book on Port Alberni, a collection of writing from the Malaspina College magazine in Nanaimo, a book on the history of B.C. religious communities, and a children's book elaborating the coast Indian figure Klee Wyck. Across the country in New Brunswick, Goose Lane Editions led off its catalogue with *Comforts of Home: Small Inns, Cottages, and Bed & Breakfasts of Atlantic Canada, Roads to Remember: The Insiders Guide to New Brunswick,* and *A Hiking Guide to the National Parks and Historic Sites of Newfoundland.*

Commodification is one of the most widespread techniques for cultural competition and survival in the new late-capitalist global economy. It is itself not new—the cultural stations of the European Grand Tour had cultural commodity value as much to the young upper-class eighteenth-century tourer recording his stops in watercolours as they do to this century's middle-class tourists with their cameras and postcards. What is new is both the participation of numerous regionalisms in self-commodification and the way in which this process has in many ways continued the regionalist displacement of political action. What has been contributing to the latter is the eclipse of national-state power by global economic institutions, and the accompanying eclipse of political institutions by economic ones. When the largest economic forces are housed outside of nation-states and their democratic institutions, the possibility of effective political participation — already problematic for the regional subject — is diminished. Citizenship becomes replaced by an emphasis on economic relations and values. Commodity acceptance in world markets becomes a source not only of regional economic prosperity, but of cultural legitimation. Regional mythologies that appear to impede the recoveries of history and politics become solidified — like Anne of Green Gables, or the festival image of Louis Riel — into saleable folklore.

One unfortunate consequence of this is that the positive force of regional affirmation — its enabling of contextually local evaluations of practices and products, including political and literary practices — is endangered by commodity fetishism. I am thinking here of Southwestern Ontario painter Greg Curnoe, whose insistence on his own regionality involved not the invention of totalizations of Southwestern Ontario, nor regional chauvinism, but rather the assertion that local particulars and practices could be invested with as much value as those particulars and practices that occur in politically or economically powerful places. Expressed as a regionalism, regional affirmation is not always friendly to the local or the particular — as the critical debate over Maritime and Atlantic representations currently shows. One of Curnoe's achievements was in being able to break Ontario-centred Canadian nationalist totalizations by asserting from both personal and family positions (like Women's Press and Sister Vision Press have done from gender and race positions) dissenting particulars which themselves leave open the possibility of further difference.

It is with these different political and cultural potentials of Canadian regional affirmation and regionalism that I will end. The two or three most successful Canadian regionalisms have historically encompassed and effaced sectionalisms and localisms (Alberta foothills, Cape Breton Island) too weak economically and institutionally to assert themselves. They have resisted and effaced rival ideological bases of identity. Yet except for

Ontario regionalism, they have also offered some ways of resisting even larger national totalizations, and in literature, with the gaining of provincial publishing infrastructures, have been able to assert alternate non-national canons and criteria for canonicity. To more fully serve the ideological diversity of the inhabitants of their regions, however, Canadian regionalisms have needed, like Curnoe's affirmations of "region" (he edited for several years an irregularly appearing journal titled *Region*), to become regionalities—open to internal differentiation by other ideologies—ideologies both of the sectional kind that provinces and powerful cities can offer, and of the transnational kind, such as gender, race, and ethnicity. As regionalities, affirmations of region can have powerful and legitimating interactions with other ideologies, helping both to historicize and contextualize them. One of Maritime scholarship's recent important contributions to the understanding of colour and race in Canada has been the identifying of the historically specific experiences of blacks in Nova Scotia from the eighteenth century onward.

Earlier literary and cultural criticisms, in their frequently uncritical acceptance of *regionalism* as a critical category, have contributed to the politically oppressive functioning of the term. Even when constructed as resistances to nation-state ideological dominants, successful Canadian regionalisms—presenting themselves as inherently natural—have become new dominants, serving particular class, race, and gender interests, and constraining social/textual dissent and change. Criticism would be well advised to treat regionalism with the same skepticism it directs toward other ideologies—substituting in its own discursive practices "regional" for "regionalist" and "regionality" for "regionalism."

Again, this is not to say that the social and geographic contexts signalled by "region" are inconsequential. To the contrary, it is because of the contextualizing and historicizing power of regional constructions that it is so important that they be discursively available outside of processes of social domination. The increasing globalization of economic power, which is being accomplished without a corresponding globalization of democratic politics, is placing an intensifying demand on regions and the constituent provinces or departments of nation-states to act as strategic political and cultural sites for democratic resistances to global assumptions. With what cultural productions are Canadians likely to be able to resist the productions of Disney, CNN, the Booker Prize, and the six or seven multinational book and video publishers that currently control 80% of the global market? With ones produced by Toronto media, productions that increasingly resemble those of the multinationals, or ones produced in Toronto suburbs and subcultures, and in Winnipeg, Moncton, St. John's, Halifax, Edmonton, Victoria, or London-Ontario? Such resistances will require regional or local effort to support regional institutions, especially theatres and magazine and book publishers, as aspects of political representation, as well as a continuation of regional efforts to acknowledge competing and intersecting ideologies and internal difference. For literary criticism such developments would make even more important the recognition that regions and places are not inevitably regionalisms but rather contexts in which specifically marked varieties of textuality differ and negotiate.

Notes

1. This is an ambiguity France has tried to create for its colonies in recreating them as overseas departments with representation in the French Chamber of Deputies and Senate—making them politically part of France while geographically and historically distinct from it.

MARJORIE PRYSE   *University at Albany, SUNY*

Writing Out of the Gap
Regionalism, Resistance, and Relational Reading

IT IS EXTREMELY DIFFICULT to imagine a common ground on which all of us—many of us from different regions, some of us from different countries—could converse about regionalism. Regionalism connotes the local, not the national—and by no means claims to represent the "universal." What we can begin by agreeing on, however, is that regionalism is not a subgenre of nature writing, although in studying regionalism, we recognize that landscape is at least as much affected by human projection and representation as some people are affected by landscape. As a preliminary definition, we might agree that regionalism represents the deep structure of local knowledge, where geographical and literary landscape become imbued and interwoven with features of culture.

In American literature, regionalism represents a tension between region and nation that manifests itself in the literary hierarchy of canonical and noncanonical authors and texts; it has, until the 1990s, relegated regionalism to the footnotes of literary history. To study literary regionalism in American literature requires an understanding of canonicity, for the two are interwoven: the cultural processes of canon and nation formation have combined to marginalize or suppress regionalist writing. The post-colonial critic and literary theorist Edward Said proposes in *Culture and Imperialism* a method of "contrapuntal reading" that allows a reader to interpret textual evidence employing a historical frame of reference outside of canonical texts; he is particularly interested in locating these texts in the context of British and European imperialism, but the method gives us a way of recognizing differences between American canonical fiction and the texts of regionalism as well. In a "contrapuntal reading," we can examine regionalist texts for evidence of an American historical frame of reference, which establishes ideologies of gender, race, class, and region; and at the same time we can examine canonical texts for evidence of the existence of alternative vision, even if such vision is mocked or parodied in the canonical text.

I will illustrate this point by setting in counterpoint and reading "contrapuntally" two American fictions from the 1880s, James's canonical novel *The Portrait of a Lady*, and Sarah Orne Jewett's regionalist story, "A White Heron." If you recall Henrietta Stackpole in *The Portrait of a Lady*, the emancipated American journalist who serves to represent for James everything that is superficial and humorous about the very idea of American women writing, you may also remember that Henrietta serves as Isabel Archer's guide to London early in the novel. Isabel is a character in search of knowledge in a large sense—but Henrietta promises her "local color" (145). For James, "local color" signifies everything that is wrong with Henrietta—and for our purposes, it serves as a sign that James is in some ways defending his own art and his own understanding of America from the predominantly female writers who were his contemporaries and who wrote regionalist fiction that moved well beyond "local color," with that term's hint of the carnival, the stereotype, the laughable. Even in this most canonical of American fictions, we find evidence of alternative vision— even though James parodies it in the character of Henrietta Stackpole.

In further counterpoint, we can examine James's young Pansy Osmond in context with Jewett's Sylvie of "A White Heron." We might term Pansy an "American girl"-in-training—a girl who views Isabel Archer as her "guardian angel" and whose characteristic feature is obedient silence. Even though Pansy, like Isabel herself, has some independence of mind, passively rejecting a suit from Lord Warburton that her father much desires, James's young character accepts the basic assumption that a girl's life is circumscribed by the social realm in which she wears ball gowns at dances where suitors present themselves (433). Jewett's Sylvie in "A White Heron" is younger than Pansy Osmond when she meets the hunter-ornithologist, who appears on her grandmother's farm with his gun, looking to shoot, stuff, and add to his collection a rare white heron. Like Pansy

Osmond, Sylvie is in the main a creature of silence and, to outward appearance, an obedient child. Also like Pansy, Sylvie passively disobeys her grandmother, her parent-surrogate, and keeps silent rather than reveal the secret of the bird's nesting place—after she has climbed the great pine-tree at dawn and "torn and tattered" her dress in the process (Fetterly and Pryse 204). Unlike Pansy, however, Sylvie reveals her resistance to their society's premises concerning her role and conduct: in refusing to share the bird's nesting place, she is also rejecting the claims of the hunter's urban wealth and privilege on her rural poverty (since the hunter has offered to pay $10 for the secret); and she even rejects heterosexuality itself, since the story implies that in order to guard the bird and implicitly her own autonomy, she must renounce her attraction for the young man. Jewett's story proposes a developmental realm for a young girl from a rural New England region that excludes the question of suitors altogether. James might have found Sylvie's choice quaint, a version of "local color"—he later praised Jewett's masterpiece, *The Country of the Pointed Firs*, as her "little quantum of achievement"—but hardly a vision of sufficient value to serve a nation in the process of figuring its own cultural representation. I, of course, would disagree with James here.

When we characterize Pansy as a girl with a measure of independence, we are examining James's novel in the historical context of the late nineteenth-century movement on behalf of women's civil rights in the U.S.; when we understand Sylvie as resisting the cultural script that creates American girls as players in heterosexual romance, we are also reading out from Jewett's story to the larger social and ideological context, here the contest over which values come to represent American vision and culture. Both are variations on contrapuntal reading, and examining these texts together illuminates the tensions and conflicts in national stories and their contrast with regional fictions, as least for American girls. In this example, regionalism preserves what national (and colonial) fictions destroy—since James views Pansy, like Isabel, as an object worthy of a collector, a daughter to be paternalistically "owned," and implicitly as a creature to be occupied and colonized, not unlike the British annexation of India, to which James makes a few symptomatic references in his novel. In "A White Heron," Sylvie herself refuses to be collected, killed and stuffed, no matter how much money is at stake—for she knows that to tell the bird's secret would be to commodify her own value. In the gap between Pansy's acceptance and Sylvie's rejection of society's basic script for the life of an American girl resides the difference between the canonical and the noncanonical, the American and the regional, the universal and the local.

My discussion of regionalism examines this gap more fully, and I argue that only when we collectively begin to understand regionalism in the context of other theories of social analysis—feminist theory, postcolonial theory, and the object relations theory that I introduce at the end of my essay—only then will we find ways to fully converse about texts that we may not share in common. For if we understand regionalism as implicitly a form of critique grounded in the local, then it becomes difficult to imagine generalizing from one regional literature to another across national borders and histories. However, Suzi Jones's notion of "regionalization," by which she means that the folkloric process can envelop imported ideologies and dress them in local costume, is really an argument about the way nationalism and imperialism work: nationalism as a process wraps hegemony in the garb of regional culture. As Francesco Loriggio points out, in an essay in David Jordan's recent volume, "regionalism . . . emerged in fiction in significant coincidence with a number of other fundamental developments: the rise of the modern nation-state and nationalism, the idea of national literature, realism, and the consolidation of European (French and British first and foremost) imperialist expansionism" (17).

The very etymology of the word *region* reminds us that regions exist within, and are subordinated by, some other rule. *Region* derives from the Latin root, *regere*, to rule—as do the words *rex* and *realm*, those rhetorical and political entities that perform the act of subordination on the region. Just as it has served the interests of nations to view regions and regional peoples as marginal to a centralizing effort and vision, in effect as internal colonies, it has also served the interest of nations to canonize writers whose work appears to produce a national literature (that is, Henry James), instead of those whose work, out of love for what a nation could and ought to be, includes a critique of dominant values in the process of constructing an alternative vision (such as Sarah Orne Jewett). Thus, again Loriggio: "regionalism has always been presented and has always presented itself as a reaction to and an offshoot of the central developments of the last two centuries, modernization and empire" (21). Loriggio's argument suggests that what we can learn from a particular regionalist literature may indeed be generalizable, at least to the extent that regionalism represents an impulse to keep alive alternative visions of national and global development. These alternative visions, like Sylvia's resistance to a commodified heterosexual bird sacrifice, reside in the gap between what Robinson Jeffers called "thickening to empire" in his poem "Shine, Perishing Republic," and a sense of possibility for cultural transformation.

I've taken the title of my essay—"writing out of the gap"—from the American philosopher of science Sandra Harding, whose own work is heavily influenced by that of Canadian sociologist Dorothy Smith. Harding and Smith are feminist "standpoint theorists" who argue that because, as Hegel and Marx asserted, "human activity, or 'material life,' not only structures but sets limits on human understanding; [the fact that] what we do shapes and constrains what we can know" (Harding 120), can help us understand why, in societies characterized by hierarchies of power and systems of domination, "the visible available to the rulers will be both partial and perverse" (Harding 120). The notion that "What we do shapes and constrains what we can know" means in part that it is to the advantage of groups in economic, political, and ideological power *not to see* the human suffering their ideas and policies create; and that on the other hand, it is essential to the survival of persons dominated and oppressed by such ideas and policies to learn as much as they can about those in power. This is an old idea in American history and culture, first raised by African-American historian W.E.B. Du Bois at the turn of the twentieth century and expressed in his phrase "double consciousness," which, he said, Americans of African descent had to develop in order to pass between black and white economic and cultural worlds.

To the extent that knowledge and canonical stories as we know them are produced by the "rulers," by dominant and nationalist ideologies about gender, race, class, and region, it follows for standpoint theorists, as it did for Du Bois, that there exists a gap, what Smith calls a "line of fault," between at least some researchers (and storytellers) and the dominant conceptual schemes. Harding argues that objectivity in science is actually increased "by thinking out of the gap between the lives of 'outsiders' and the lives of 'insiders' and their favoured conceptual schemes" (Harding 132), and I would extend this concept to the literary as well. Because the gap itself is experienced primarily by "outsiders," these "outsiders" ("regionals," in terms of the present discussion) have access to what some theorists have termed "epistemic privilege"—Du Bois's "double consciousness"; that is, they see their own positions as well as the contradictions between those positions and dominant ideologies. Whereas the thinking and stories of "insiders" have nothing to gain by recognizing the contradictions and therefore such stories, what often become "canonical" fictions, mute even the possibility of literary and knowledge production from the gap: once again, in Harding's words, "the vision available to the rulers will be both partial and perverse." We could say that regionalism represents in narrative a sense of place that reflects a gap between dominant ideological and aesthetic interests and the interests and stories of persons who reside in the locale. Regionalism becomes, in effect, writing out of that gap, and regionalist writers construct "place" as cultural, economic, geographical, and political "position," or, to use a more theoretical word, "standpoint."

In one of the clearest statements of standpoint epistemology a century before the writings of Dorothy Smith and Sandra Harding, the New England regionalist Mary Wilkins Freeman, in "A Church Mouse," expressed the idea that, in effect, "what we do shapes what we can know." Writing of her poor, homeless, unemployed, unmarried, and old character, Hetty Fifield, whose desperation leads her to challenge her New England village's gender codes that bar women from the position of sexton and to move her meagre furniture into the meeting-house, in effect hiring herself as sexton by occupying the church, Freeman's narrator observes, "When one is hard pressed, one, however simple, gets wisdom as to vantage-points" (Fetterly and Pryse 349). Hetty Fifield decorates the sanctuary with her own worsted work, hangs a sunflower quilt around the hearth, and, by turning the meeting house into a human habitation, raises the moral question of her own homelessness. Although it is initially the village's women who precipitate Hetty's eviction from the church the day they arrive for meeting and smell the odours from her previous evening's cabbage dinner, it is also the women who subsequently block that eviction by the church fathers, an event presented as an image of violation, recognizing in Hetty's plight their own future. Readers who have experienced the economic gap of being closed out of certain jobs and rendered dependent on patriarchal structures for survival will recognize "A Church Mouse" as a bold resistance narrative, even if Freeman ends by invoking the Christmas spirit to explain the village's eventual charity towards Hetty Fifield—thereby increasing the market-value of her fiction for the periodicals who published her in the 1880s. What Freeman knew a century ago is that oppressed groups develop, out of that very oppression, "epistemic privilege"—what Freeman terms "vantage points" and what we know as "standpoint epistemology."

With Freeman as our touchstone, we can understand nineteenth-century and early twentieth-century American literary regionalism as telling the story of the marginalized "other," written from the regions with a standpoint consciously defined against the dominant reading of "others," signified as regionals in these works. The dominant reading, explicit or implicit in the texts of regionalism, and epitomized in part by the "local color" approach to writing about regional characters, views persons and assigns them value (or devalues them) according to hierarchical cultural discourses about gender, class, race, age, physical ability, and marital status as well as region. Within the texts of regionalism, however, narrators and regional characters resist this dominant reading, muting its silencing effect, and teach readers how to approach "others" differently. (I've written about how this works in particular texts, and for the classroom, in my "Reading Regionalism: The 'Difference' It Makes.") Regionals, in these narratives, derive a certain immunity from genuine scrutiny by their high-cultural contemporaries precisely because they are viewed, by outsiders, as stereotypes or stock figures, thus creating a gap between regionals' self-representation and their representation in dominant cultural narratives. Feminist standpoint epistemology offers us particular clarification in understanding regionalism because it reminds us that the stories dominant cultures have told themselves about gender, race, class, and region can only represent, in Harding's words, a "partial and perverse" vision.

In many works of American literature, regional characters serve the function of humor for condescending urbanities, or for wealthy, white, and often male readers (as did the portraits of rural male characters, and women, in the fiction of the "humorists of the Old Southwest"). However, in regionalist texts, regional characters engage in acts of resistance that challenge their definition, and dismissal, by writers more in the mainstream, or aspiring to be. As I have written in "Reading Regionalism," "regionalist texts construct a critique of the subordinate positions created for, then occupied by, rural, elderly, poor, female, un- or unconventionally married, often untutored persons" (50). The narratives collected in *American Women Regionalists* and other regionalist texts share a rhetorical awareness of the role of region, for the dominant culture, in creating and maintaining hierarchies based on the other excluding discourses of gender, race, and class. Writing under the sign of region, then, gives writers in the regionalist mode a rhetorical space, an epistemological and cultural standpoint "within" the dismissal of region as a base for power or culture that the very etymology of the word records.

Regionalists approach narratives of place differently than other writers literary history has also loosely termed "regional." In the American nineteenth century, such allusions to region, in the works of writers like James Fenimore Cooper, George Washington Harris, Samuel Clemens, and William Dean Howells, often reinscribe the ideological assumptions that subordinated not only regional male characters, but also Native Americans, African Americans, and women. Far from opposing stereotypes based on race, gender, or region, these writers produced fictions that supported subordinating hierarchies. However, region, in the texts predominantly by women regionalists (but including some male writers, such as Charles Chesnutt or, as Peter Vaccavari notes in Jordan's volume, Albion Tourgee), becomes much more than a geographical representation. For even though the literal topography of place matters for some of the regionalists, especially Celia Thaxter and Mary Austin, the texts are not "about" place in a literal sense. Rather, "geographical region" stands in the same relation to "regionalism" as "female" stands to "feminism": "region" and "female" are naturalizing terms, but they do not serve as the essences of regionalism or feminism. Indeed, the tendency for most nineteenth-century American fiction to support the hierarchies (offering only portraits of male artists as dissenting voices) has led Judith Fetterley, in a recent issue of *College English*, to wonder whether the regionalists are "American" writers at all to the extent that American literature creates as its primary plot putting people in their places according to hierarchies of gender, race, class, and region. The texts of regionalism refuse to be plotted: they refuse to take on the forms, characters, stories, and outcomes that characterize "American" fiction. If *to narrate* is *to rule*, they write prose that "orders" itself, is ruled, as little as possible by hierarchies of dominance and value—and indeed, the narrative form of most regionalist writing focuses on character and sketch. These are not stories with an ending in the conventional sense.

If regionalism's *point of view* may be considered standpoint epistemology, the particular "vantage-points" regional characters derive from their position, then the particular *aesthetic* of regionalism, its appeal to readers a century ago as well as today, becomes a narrative of resistance—an appeal similar to that evoked by postcolonialist fictions in a global context. Although I am focusing in this essay on American literature, I will offer one example from postcolonial texts. Tsitsi Dangarembga's 1988 *Nervous Conditions* is an autobiographical first novel by a Zimbabwean woman whose protagonist is a poor, rural, young girl, and a great deal of the story takes place at home or in school with other rural and female students. Dangarembga's *bildungsroman* tells the story of her protagonist's growing awareness of sexism in Zimbabwean culture and family life, interwoven with the neocolonialism of Zimbabwean patriarchy and her own internalized classism and colonialism as she becomes educationally privileged, scoring high enough on a test to win a place in an English-run private boarding school in which she discovers the extent of her Africanness—through her experiences of social exclusion—for the first time. Like its nineteenth-century American counterparts that often covered over their resistance with humour, rusticity, or happy endings (such as the Christmas ending of "A Church Mouse"), Dangarembga's novel has as its "cover" the fact that it is not about politics, or even overtly about development and internalized racism, but "only" a story about a rural girl in a culture she characterizes as distinctly uninterested in rural female children. I do not know whether Zimbabwe has a concept of a national literature, but if it does, *Nervous Conditions* writes from the regions. Dangarembga and the American regionalists create resistance narrators, "coding" their fictions (as in Emily Dickinson's famous lines, "Tell all the Truth but tell it slant"), so that readers with "partial and perverse vision," readers taught the ideologies of dominance and nation, will either not notice the subversiveness of these narratives at all, or perhaps, in efforts to contain their potential power, trivialize them with phrases such as "local color," "regional realism," or, in the 1990s, "noncanonical."

Specific examples of regionalism as resistance literature include Charles Waddell Chesnutt's stories from *The Conjure Woman*, in which he was able to create "humorous" fictions about white-black relations that on the one hand did not "offend" conservative white readers (because the stories are open to the dominant interpretation that Uncle Julius, their narrator, is a "foolish" former slave) and yet at the same time created the possibility that the "joke" is really on the segregationists. Chesnutt created a strategy for writing resistance narratives that would be recognizable to readers who were sympathetic with the experience of the gap racial segregation created, but at the same time would not incur the wrath of editors, publishers, and readers who held to the dominant ideology about the proper "place" for Americans of African descent.

For many of the writers in *American Women Regionalists*, regionalist narrative provided a strategy of concealment as well as of resistance. Alice Dunbar-Nelson, who wrote about Creole culture in New Orleans, provides an excellent example of a writer who was explicitly informed by her editor, Bliss Perry, that the American public had a "'dislike' for treatment of 'the color-line'" (*Color* 57), and who therefore rarely identified her fictional characters as persons of colour. Yet in the mode of writing from a region, Dunbar-Nelson was able to tell stories about social and cultural hierarchies similar enough to those of turn-of-the-century race relations that she was then free to explore as long as she did not explicitly link "regional" and "Creole" with "Negro."

Her story "The Goodness of St. Rocque" provides an example. In this story, dark-eyed and dark-haired Manuela loses Theophile, whom she considers her own, to the blonde, petite Claralie. While Claralie makes novenas at the shrine of St. Rocque, an acceptable way of praying to influence outcomes, Manuela visits the Wizened One, a shriveled, elderly, and "yellow" (read "of African descent") woman who has access to charms not sanctioned in the Catholic Church. By following the advice of the Wizened One, Manuela wins Theophile back. Within a frame that can be read as "local color," Dunbar-Nelson explores the politics of colourism and class within the Creole community and authorizes the implicitly Voodoo culture of the Wizened One. The light-dark contrast in the rivalry between Claralie and Manuela is resolved to Manuela's triumph; but the real "triumph," like that of Charles Chesnutt, is over those readers willing to read "local color" but not about race.

In Mary Austin's story "The Walking Woman," the narrator portrays an unconventional Western homeless wanderer, a woman who has "walked off all sense of society-made values" (582). She is interested in the Walking Woman because she has "passed unarmed and offended" (578) through the Western desert: "by no canon could it be considered ladylike to go about on your own feet, with a blanket and a black bag and almost no money in your purse, in and about the haunts of rude and solitary men" (578). When she hears the woman's story of free love with an itinerant shepherd and joyous birth of a child, however, she experiences a moment of "fullest understanding" with the Walking Woman—"it was the naked thing the Walking Woman grasped, not dressed and tricked out . . . by prejudices . . ." (582). And when the narrator sees the woman others have described as lame disappear from the camp, she runs to trace the footsteps she has left: "there in the bare, hot sand the track of her two feet bore evenly and white" (583). Setting up a contrast between Maverick and Mayfair, between Walking Woman's freedom and London fashion, Austin's story of Western life takes as its emblem of region a woman who violates the "canon" of "ladylike" conduct.

Resistance narratives make it possible to read meanings of the experiences of regional women and nondominant men in "alter"ing ways. Dominant cultural reading practices create internal censors designed to block such ways of reading and meaning-making. As Sandra Harding writes,

> what we can see in the world around us is a function not just of what is there plus our individual talents and skills but of how our society designs the cultural filters through which we observe the world around and within us and how it institutionalizes those filters in ways that leave them invisible to individuals. (116)

Designed to prevent seeing, the "cultural filters" that Harding describes, and that regionalist narratives resist, only work when they themselves remain invisible to readers. Once writing out of the gap reveals the existence and power of the filters, not only do they become visible but it becomes possible to imagine a world of "local" knowledge they have hidden, and to explore and "construct" that world.

By what process does writing from the gap make us as readers aware of differences once obscured by cultural filters, and in particular to begin to recognize ourselves as "other" and as "regional"? Just as standpoint epistemology gives us a framework for understanding regionalism as narratives of position, object relations, a theory of the "pre-Oedipal" phase in human psychosocial development, can help us understand how resistance narratives affect readers. In the sense that regions "precede" nation, we could say that they also represent a "pre-Oedipal" phase in the development of nation. In order to understand the effects of keeping alive regional memory and alternative vision of community through a regionalist critique and simultaneous creation of regionals as characters worthy of respect, I will turn briefly to object relations theory, specifically the work of Melanie

Klein and D.W. Winnicott, along with the work of ego psychologist Margaret Mahler, in order to describe the "relational reading" process that regionalism as resistance narrative elicits.

For Klein, it is not the phallus that "represents" cultural and symbolic order but the breast, the part-object that both feeds the child and serves as a bridge to culture. Mahler used the term "attunement" to describe the learned mutuality and reciprocity between infant and caretaker. And Winnicott gave us the well-known phrase the "good-enough mother" to describe the response of a caretaker who "understands" what the infant "needs." Klein in particular allows us to imagine that the infant is "reader," interpreting the movements of what she calls the "part-object," the "breast" (loosely referential for what and whoever literally feeds the infant), from the infant's position of physical powerlessness. Before the infant has any text to "write" other than naked need, it "reads" for its survival; and it reads in emerging relationship with an adult caretaker who has the capability to identify what we might call the infant's standpoint, to learn what the infant "knows," and to "read" in attunement with the infant's world from this standpoint.

Any theory of reading that emerges from the combined perspective of object relations theory and feminist standpoint theory must address the "attunement" that resistance narratives can create for readers who have been taught to read through the "cultural filters" of dominant ideologies about gender, race, class, and region—but who have not felt "mothered" but rather stunted and alienated by them. Indeed, cultural stories that have reinforced hierarchies of value (most canonical fictions), in which women, nondominant men, and regional people live life at the bottom and are viewed as undeserving of resources, power, or opportunities, have failed at attunement. Such stories and the ideologies from which they derive have created instead what Melanie Klein called rage and a desire to kill in segments of the devalued population; these cultural texts, whether written or unwritten, have not served as a "good-enough mother." Writing from the gap, however, is an *intentional* attempt to "take care" of such stunted, alienated, and enraged—because dispossessed—readers, and to the extent that regionalist narratives attempt to resist dominant ideologies, readers who live in the gap may interpret their "intentions" as reparative, reconstructive, and empowering. Recalling that the etymology of the word "intention" derives from the Latin *intendere*, "to stretch toward," we can view the resistance of regionalist narratives as "intending" or "stretching toward" those whose cultural expressions have remained unrecognized and unrewarded by a society designed to accumulate capital, power, and control over knowledge for the exclusive enjoyment and use of a privileged few.

Such intentionality (a word that I am aware violates critical taboos) extends to a literary context the concept of the "good-enough mother," or Winnicott's related concept of the "nursing couple," which implies reciprocity between infant and caretaker. The relationship between a cultural text and its reader creates the possibility of a "reading couple" to the extent that the text imagines writing *out* of the gap for readers who live *in* the gap—where this gap between dominant ideologies and the experiences of women, nondominant men, and cultural "others" becomes the cultural cartography of region.

Narrators of such regionalist texts postulate readers who are culturally deprived to the extent that national and canonical stories lack attunement with their regional, women, and minority readers, thereby failing to "feed" these readers in their development as cultural subjects. For such readers, access to "alter"-narratives promotes the development of an alternative culture—a culture comprised of subjects who have been sustained, "mothered" if you will, by "other" narrators than those sanctioned by what we know at present as "dominant" culture. Such a process rests on critique of the dominant culture and its material practices; it also fosters construct of a standpoint epistemology, a knowledge based on the perspectives of persons who gain, through regionalism, access to "good-enough (cultural) mothering." Indeed, "mothering" for a reparative culture requires "othering," if by that term we mean the internalized capacity to see and feel *with* the "other," to experience the self as seen and felt *by* "others," and in short, to achieve the empathy that Melanie Klein identified as the gain once the infant manages to move beyond rage at the withholding breast and to wish to make reparations *to* the breast. Neither the infant nor the culturally deprived subject can thrive without the reaching out, the "intention," of a "(m)other" and a "(m)othering culture."

Reclaiming our ability to recall counter-hegemonic cultural values requires us as readers to reconnect with what object relations theorists term the "good object." This is the ultimate theoretical significance of reclaiming a "sense of place": region becomes the "good object" in a cultural application of object relations. Through specific acts of reading in which the texts themselves "reach out" to culturally deprived and dispossessed subjects, readers can learn to resist internalizing narrators and narratives that abuse or ignore them—a process Judith Fetterley implicitly described twenty years ago as characteristic of the "resisting reader." Such acts, in which regionalism among other resistance narratives participates as one member of a "reading couple," allow readers to move beyond murderous rage and towards reparation, to imagine and to work to create a society constructed out of critique, but attuned to the needs of its human members.

If resistance serves as the displaced "plot" of regionalism, then, relationship becomes the strategy by which the texts of regionalism create a community of readers. The pervasive reliance on dialogue—and dialect—which characterizes many of the texts of regionalism itself suggests this body of work as a form of conversation between regionalist narrators and readers, as an act of social and cultural intercourse, a coupling by reading. Regionalists build readers into their texts as collaborators in the practice of revaluing and re-viewing both the regional subjects themselves and their relevance, in some historical present sense, to readers a century or more later. The texts of regionalism bring readers close, encourage "close reading"; when Jewett's narrator in *The Country of the Pointed Firs* sits down in Mrs. Blackett's rocking chair in order to see the Green Island woman's view of sky and sea, the text invites its own reader to do the same—identifying closeness or empathy as one way of listening to the voices and values of marginalized and regionalized people and places.

The term "close reading" may, for some, evoke a New Critical myopia. Developments in literary theory during the past twenty years have discredited formalism and techniques of "close reading" as the New Critics defined them; and yet, the texts of regionalism ask us to reconsider the meaning of "close" reading and to redefine its usefulness. The texts of regionalism suggest that immersion in "different" narratives requires skills that involve a new kind of close reading: reading closely, with attention to particulars and to "peculiars"; reading within the self-contained centre of a writer's standpoint or cultural or regional position; and reading with a decision to sit in Mrs. Blackett's rocking chair, to read with human closeness and connection, to empathize if possible—and, where empathy would be disrespectful, as in Mary Austin's portrait of the Native American woman Seyavi in "The Basket Maker," to maintain appropriate distance.

The texts of regionalism also convey closeness between narrator and subject of narration. In some cases—the writings of Alice Cary and Zitkala-Sä serve as examples—narrators themselves are also regional subjects. In others—works by Mary Noialles Murfree and Sarah Orne Jewett—

narrators enter the region as sympathetic outsiders. In either case, implicit in the approach of narrators to their subjects is the belief that readers are taught, changed, and recreated by the stories they read. The theoretical "text" of regionalism may actually "take place," produce a "sense of place," in the process of interaction that characterizes the relationship between reader and text; the "reading couple" becomes part of regionalism's textuality.

This is not to say that regionalism makes for easy reading. On the contrary. The sexism, racism, and classism that have come to characterize American national culture have taught us to "read" both social and American natural worlds in a certain way. This particular socialization of our reading practices has obscured our ability to engage in a genuine dialogue with the social and natural world unmediated by hierarchies of gender, race, class, and region. The regionalists do not assume that the existence of these hierarchies is inevitable, and therefore, upon entering the individual texts that form the mosaic of regionalism, readers often find themselves in uncertain territory, encountering characters who do not even speak in "standard" or literary English—or Spanish, or French. The narratives of regionalism emerge from a different social world than the one we have been taught in conventional ways to "read."

Thus the "reading couple" in regionalism takes multiple forms. In one way, it represents the relationship between the regionalist narrator and her or his fictional subjects; in another, it creates a relationship between the narrator and a prospective reader; in still another, it implies that the act of narration is itself a mediated form of reading intended to connect the reader of the text with the process of learning to read "differently." In reading regionalism, perhaps because no paradigm currently exists to "fit" regionalism into American literary history except to confuse it with "local color" and marginalize it as "regional realism," we encounter texts that criticism has not yet mediated for us. We enter into a form of "object relation" with these texts; and to the extent that they continue to offer a cultural critique, they "(m)other" us. They help us discover our capacity for reading "otherwise," as Shoshana Felman puts it (157-59). We read in close relation to persons from regions different from our own; and we read ourselves back, discovering in the works of white women early on, then both white women and women and men of colour later in the tradition, that regionalism creates an opening for ongoing dialogue about reading "differently" and for critique of a national culture that has rendered invisible so much of

American experience—more fully gendered, regionalized, coloured, enriched, and enabled by critical efforts in our own historical present time.

DAVID MARTIN　　　　　　　　　　*University of Minnesota*

"Regionalist" Fiction and the Problem of Cultural Knowledge

REGIONALISM AND ANTHROPOLOGY share deep ties. "Regionalist" literature, as many now describe it, is not just the expression of local influences or local affiliations. Rather, because "region" itself implies a cultural subdivision of some larger realm, regionalist literature has a comparative dimension. As David Jordan writes, "In examining borders that define difference, the regionalist author encounters confrontations not only along geographic borders that contain distinct local artefacts, but also along epistemological borders that define a particular sense of place, [and] cultural borders that separate a distinct regional community from the larger society within which it exists" (10). Writing across cultural as well as topographic boundaries, regionalist literature sounds much like ethnography. Indeed, as James D. Hart observes, regionalism emphasizes "basic philosophical or sociological distinctions which the writer often views as though he were a cultural anthropologist" (632).

This way of understanding regionalist literature—as performing an ethnographic function through fictional means—promises to give regionalism new relevance and cogency. If region can be understood "as the spatial dimension of cultural pluralism" (Steiner and Mondale x), then regionalism, by modeling a way of writing across cultural divides, speaks to pressing issues of cultural identity, difference, and heterogeneity. But this way of understanding regionalism leaves too much about its kinship with anthropology unexplored—particularly since anthropology's own role in managing cultural diversity has sparked such energetic debate.[1] If "regionalism" derives value from adopting an anthropological mission, it also adopts some of the fundamental problems that anthropology grapples with—problems about the nature and significance of "cultural knowledge."

These problems emerge with particular clarity in the regionalist movement of the late nineteenth-century United States—in the work of Sarah Orne Jewett, Hamlin Garland, George Washington Cable, Mary Wilkins Freeman, Constance Fenimore Woolson, Joel Chandler Harris, and others of the "local colour" genre. It has become more common to call most of these writers "regionalists" rather than "local colourists," since to many critics "local colour" implies a view of regional life from the "outside" and an attitude of condescension toward it, while "regionalism" implies a view of regional life from the "inside" and an attitude of sympathy toward it.[2] I retain the term "local colour" in this paper partly as a convenient way of denoting this particular regionalist movement, as opposed to regionalist writing in general, and partly to suspend the distinction between "inside" and "outside" perspectives, between "condescending" and "sympathetic" approaches, in the interest of working toward more productive ways of describing regionalist intentionalities.

Indeed, in this movement, the kinship between regionalism and anthropology is particularly strong. In his recent book *Cultures of Letters*, Richard Brodhead argues that we should see these writers in the context of what he calls "touristic or vacationistic prose" (125): they participate in a "concerted textual program" that "gave exercise to a sophisticate-vacationer's habits of mind" (133). While this is on the right track, it is more accurate, I think, to read the "local colourists" alongside the emerging ethnography, or protoethnography, of their time: accounts of the great Western surveys, the folklore of Mary Eastman, the ethnologies of Frank Cushing and Alice Fletcher, and just about all the anthropological writing before Franz Boas and his disciples re-invented the field at the turn of the century.[3]

In the literary economy of their time, in fact, local colour fiction and anthropological writing are inextricably mixed. Between the Civil War and the end of the century, they often appeared side by side in the same journals, reaching similar audiences and appealing to similar interests. In 1871, for example, *The Atlantic Monthly* ran Clarence King's proto-ethnographic expedition accounts interspersed with local-colour fiction by Bret Harte. In 1882, it printed Frank Cushing's report on the Zuñi among stories by Sarah Orne Jewett and Rose Terry Cooke. In 1894, *Century* magazine ran Alice Fletcher's studies of the Omaha along with stories by Jewett, Joel Chandler Harris, Kate Chopin, and Charles Egbert Craddock. Paging through a late-nineteenth-century American periodical, one sees a smooth continuum of writing about American cultures, ranging from the purely scientific to the purely imaginative, from treatments of exotic peoples to treatments of nearby communities. Sometimes, as in George Washington Cable's four-part series on Creole life and Louisiana history in *Century*, or in the *Atlantic*'s unsigned "Studies in the South" series, the boundary between "local colour" and ethnography grows virtually indistinguishable. In the literary culture of the time, local colour fiction and anthropological writing appear as nearby points, often complementary points, and sometimes inseparable points on a single line.

There is a perfectly good reason for this: local colour writing holds a deep functional affinity with ethnography. The local colourists' recurrent interests parallel those of their anthropological contemporaries. A similar concern for the oral narrative—for storytelling and for the stories that circulate in specific cultures—underlies both the anthropologist's interest in folklore and the local colourist's predilection for framed narrative. By the same token, contemporary anthropology's taxonomies of aboriginal languages and local colour's fascination with dialect show a shared interest in linguistic diversity.[4] For their central dramas, both local colour and ethnography zero in on ritual events such as funerals, religious events, and entertainment customs. All in all, local colour is less about regional *settings* than regional *societies*. In 1871, anthropologist E.B. Tylor defined "culture" as "that complex whole which includes knowledge, belief, art, morals, law, custom, and any other capabilities and habits acquired by man as a member of society" (qtd. in Mark, 109). The main subject matter of local colour fiction is regional "culture," in Tylor's sense of the term.[5]

Even more important is the kind of gaze—a distinctly anthropological one—that local colour turns on the regional cultures it portrays. A local colour story does not just portray the life of a Maine village, a mining settlement, or a Bayou community; it tries to render the inner logic of these places—what the people are like, how they live, and why. If a regionalist story has done its job, then when you put it down, you should feel that you *know* something about that region. One representative example of the kind of comment that peppers the critical record on these writers comes from Carlos Baker, who remarks that "one finishes books like [Craddock's] *The Prophet of the Great Smoky Mountains* (1885) and *In the 'Stranger People's' Country* (1895) with an authoritative knowledge of backwoods life in Tennessee during the Reconstruction period" (851). This fiction may try to preserve some of the foreignness—the difference—of the places it depicts, but it also tries to render these places intelligible. In local colour fiction, regional culture is the object of scrutiny, of analysis, and of interpretation.

The regionalist fiction of the late nineteenth-century United States, in short, has a strongly ethnographic dimension. Because of its ethnographic dimension, local colour inevitably finds itself formulating and responding to issues traditionally associated with anthropology. Some of these issues are conceptual: What, exactly, does it mean to "understand" a culture? Is this understanding reserved only for members, or can a cultural "outsider" achieve it? How does one attain both a properly "objective" understanding of a culture and a deeply intersubjective one? How, that is, does one both retain distance and "go native"—the classic paradox of the anthropological method?

Political and ethical questions arise, too. What are the ramifications of making a regional culture the object of knowledge? Because knowledge never comes about in a social vacuum, relations of knowledge between one culture and another inevitably engage relations of power. Knowing an alien culture can be a way of asserting one's power over it, especially when knowledge is acquired through force, when it is put to imperialistic ends, or when it subordinates the observed material to imposed frames of reference. But knowing an alien culture can also be a form of submission to it, especially when one's desire to know is baffled, when one becomes dependent on local sources of information, or when one must alter or assimilate to a culture in order to know it.

Nearly all of the local colourists wrote stories allegorizing local colour's own anthropological project in what I will call "ethnographic subplots." These subplots embody the anthropological impulse in the figure of an observer, either a character or a narrative persona who looks on and tries to understand a regional community. As the story follows this observer's progress, it embodies the anthropological hermeneutic in its basic narrative form, in the movement of the observer's consciousness toward an understanding of the regional life he or she confronts.

Sarah Orne Jewett's *Deephaven* provides a model of this subplot. Underneath its episodic surface narrative runs a consistent, linear narrative about two observers: Helen, whose last name is unspecified, and Kate Lancaster, her companion. At the narrative's opening, these observers take a distant and marginal position with respect to the community of Deephaven. On vacation from Boston for the summer, they expect it to be "dull in Deephaven for two young ladies who were fond of gay society and dependent upon excitement" (8), and so they put all their energy into "jolly housekeeping" (10), interacting as little as possible with Deephaven itself. Then they embark on a quest to get to know this community. They cast themselves as folklorists, cultivating acquaintances with the village elders to learn its history, traditions, and superstitions. They cast themselves as archaeologists who excavate the latent meaning below Deephaven's surface, the meaning buried in the faded inscriptions on headstones, vacant warehouses, old desk drawers, even the faces and speech of the residents, who "looked as if they must be . . . exact copies of their remote ancestors" (44-5). They cast themselves as pupils of local ways, such as knot-tying, weather-reading, and deep-sea fishing. By the end of the book, these methods have paid off: Helen and Kate are adopted members of the community, and claim an intimate knowledge of Deephaven's character, its society, its history. They compliment themselves on how they "became in the course of time learned in all manner of 'longshore lore'" (139), and on their "importance as members of society" (140); having gained an insider's knowledge of Deephaven, they can speak about it with authority.

This is the classic trajectory of the ethnographic subplot. Roughly paralleling what Dilthey called the "hermeneutic circle," it traces the processes of observation, interpretation, and assimilation that lead toward knowledge. In these ethnographic subplots, the local colourists explore the implications of what it means to make a regional culture the object of knowledge. They grapple with the conceptual and political questions that arise naturally from the ethnographic dimension of their fictions: what "cultural knowledge" consists of, how it can be obtained, and how it can serve as a means of domination or self-critique.

Ethnographic subplots like this are common in local colour fiction. What do they tell us about cultural knowledge? The first thing to notice is a deep ambivalence. On the surface, these works usually portray the process of getting to know a regional culture as a passive, innocent, and benign effort. But the subtext typically tells a different story. The observer appears as a kind of infiltrator, and his or her efforts to acquire cultural knowledge appear as a form of conquest.

Jewett's *Deephaven* again offers a paradigmatic example. Helen and Kate's investigative efforts seem, at first blush, so wholesome, motivated by genuine sympathy at best, puckish curiosity at worst. But Jewett also portrays their efforts as a species of infiltration. When Deephaven's residents balk at divulging their secrets, as when Captain Sands appears unwilling to talk about superstition (93-5), Helen and Kate pry it out of them. When Deephaven society does not open up to their scrutiny, Helen and Kate resort to eavesdropping—as, for example, with the recalcitrant group of old sea-captains. "We used to wish we could join this agreeable company," Helen reports, "but we found that the appearance of an outsider caused a disapproving silence, and that the meeting was evidently not to be interfered with" (49). So to hear this "inconceivably edifying" conversation, the girls become "impertinent enough to hide . . . just round the corner of the warehouse" (49). On a visit to Miss Chauncey, one of Deephaven's many elderly residents, Kate worries that they may be turned away, so she proposes that they "go in and look around the lower rooms" first in her absence (128). Helen and Kate's investigations are subtly intrusive maneuvers in a muted contest for knowledge.

George Washington Cable's "'Tite Poulette" shows the intrusive side of the observer's efforts even more emphatically. Kristian Koppig, a young Dutchman in New Orleans, takes an interest in the Creole women who live across the street. He wants to help them, and finds that to be of any use, he must come to terms with New Orleans' cultural fabric: its rituals, its norms, its baroque codes of conduct.

On the surface, Koppig's anthropological impulse seems wholly disinterested. But at the same time, he is also an infiltrator. From the story's outset, Kristian Koppig is cast as an invader, "one of that army of gentlemen who, after the purchase of Louisiana, swarmed from all parts of the commercial world, over the mountains of Franco-Spanish exclusiveness, like the Goths over the Pyrenees, and settled down in New Orleans to pick up their fortunes, with the diligence of hungry pigeons" (155). And from the moment of his arrival, Koppig is cast as a spy: he "made his home in a room with one dormer window looking out, and somewhat down, upon a building opposite," the building where Poulette and Madame John live (155).

Koppig spies almost constantly, staying home "with his window darkened for the very purpose" of glimpsing Poulette (160). Throughout the story the walls of Poulette's house signify a barrier that men try to penetrate, both bodily and visually. In this light, Koppig's interest in the Creole women, his ostensibly protective and benevolent surveillance, appears voyeuristic and invasive.

This notion—that the process of coming to know a regional culture is a process of infiltration—forms a persistent undertow in many ethnographic subplots. Indeed, this implication lies buried in many of our common terms for understanding: one "gets underneath," "apprehends," "catches," "seizes," "unravels," or "penetrates" what one comes to know. All the military (and often sexual) connotations of these locutions resonate strongly in local colour fiction. The observer, attempting to intellectually "penetrate" a regional culture, is always, latently, a spy or infiltrator. As a result, ethnographic subplots enact battles for intellectual access, foregrounding the sense of conquest lurking beneath a superficially benign curiosity about other regions.

The uneasiness of the local colourists toward their own anthropological dimension shows up in another way, too. This way regards how they portray the end-point, the goal, of all this investigation: the knowledge or understanding it yields. Cultural understanding establishes a particular relationship between the observer and the regional culture he or she observes. What is the nature of this relationship? With this question, too, local colour often presents superficially rosy answers. Understanding, these works suggest, allows sympathy, which in turn establishes a relationship of harmony and benevolence. In Deephaven, for example, Helen's understanding allows her to put aside her biases and appreciate the village on its own terms: "It is wonderful, the romance and tragedy and adventure which one may find in a quiet old-fashioned country town, though to heartily enjoy the every-day life one must care to study life and character, and must find pleasure in thought and observation of simple things, and have an instinctive, delicious interest in what to other eyes is unflavored dullness" (37).

Understanding, Jewett suggests, establishes a plane of identification and sympathy. It overcomes regional antagonisms. This is often held out as a positive model for the sort of cultural knowledge that local colour's anthropological characters seek. In Joel Chandler Harris's "Azalia," for example, as the Northern characters come to understand the Southern ones better, "the last barrier of sectional reserve (if it may be so termed) was broken down.... In the language of the little rector, 'all things became homogeneous through the medium of sympathy and the knowledge of mutual suffering'" (302). In Woolson's "In the Cotton Country," the narrator's endeavor to understand the South makes her better able to sympathize and to help: "In time," she says, "I succeeded in building up a sort of friendship with this solitary woman of the waste, and in time she told me her story.... [S]hall we not, we women, like Sisters of Charity, go over the field when the battle is done, bearing balm and wine and oil for those who suffer?" (184).

As these texts portray it, cultural knowledge neutralizes and compensates for political conflict. This is, in fact, the common praise for local colour's anthropological impulse, its effort to generate and purvey knowledge about America's regional life. Claude Simpson, for example, writes in the introduction to his popular anthology of local colour fiction that after the Civil War

> the difference between legal unity and cultural diversity was as great as ever, and many persons seem to have felt a pressing need for a depth of understanding that slogans and propaganda had made impossible during the conflict.... Thus the psychological need to interpret local characters, local geography, local fauna and flora, local idiom and folkways seems to underlie the impulse that kept a generation of essayists and storytellers busy. (5-6)

Understanding leads to harmony. Deep down, though, the local colourists seem skeptical of this proposition. They persistently imply that cultural understanding amounts to appropriation: one "gets," "grasps," or "seizes" what one understands. Jewett grapples with this possibility throughout her writing, returning to it in "William's Wedding," her posthumously published coda to *The Country of the Pointed Firs*. The narrator describes an epiphany, a moment when, "only because [she] came to know them ... in their own habitations," she sees clearly "the simple natures" of Mrs. Blackett, William Blackett and Mrs. Todd. On the surface, this understanding appears entirely salutary: having "lived in Dunnet until the usual distractions and artifices of the world were no longer in control," she finds "love in its simplicity." But, again, understanding amounts to possession. This account, the narrator explains, is "written for those who have a Dunnet Landing of their own: who either kindly share this with its writer, or possess another." Dunnet Landing has become property. And while understanding allows the narrator to see Dunnet's residents clearly, it also transforms them into interchangeable, transferable objects: the counterparts of Mrs. Blackett, Mrs. Todd, and William "are in every village in the world, thank heaven" (559-60).

To know something is to "get" it. Constance Woolson's "In the Cotton Country" provides a forceful demonstration of how knowledge can amount to intellectual appropriation. The story's embedded narrative sketches the life of Judith Kinsolving, a Southern woman impoverished and embittered by the Civil War. The story's frame narrative tells of how the story's unnamed narrator, a visiting observer, comes to understand Judith and, through her, Southern hardship and resentment.

On one level, "Cotton Country" implies that knowledge enables sympathy, appreciation, and harmony—it allows "we women" to become "Sisters of Charity . . . bearing balm and wine and oil for those who suffer" (184). On another level, though, "Cotton Country" implies that the narrator's understanding acts as a form of appropriation. It does this by asking us to question the frame-narrator's motives, and to see how her "understanding" of Judith Kinsolving serves her own needs.

Subtly but clearly, Woolson reveals the creepy, compulsive side of this narrator's activity, her stance toward the South, and her efforts to understand what she sees. When she comes across a lone and decrepit house, she becomes evasive about her response. "Two houses are sociable and commonplace" she explains; "but one all alone on a desolate waste like that inspired me with—let us call it interest" (181). What else, Woolson teases us, might we call it? This eerie curiosity surfaces again when the narrator comes upon Judith Kinsolving, the occupant of this lone house: "The woman's face baffled me," the narrator says, "and I do not like to be baffled" (182). This drives the narrator to compulsive efforts, causing her to wait "impatiently for the hour when [she] could enter into the presence of [Judith's] great silence." But she is further rebuffed: "How still she was! If she had wept, if she had raved, if she had worked with nervous energy, or been resolutely, doggedly idle, if she had seemed reckless, or callous, or even pious; but no, she was none of these" (183). The narrator has to stifle the impulse to interrogate Judith: "I could not very well say, 'Who are you, and how came you here?' and yet that was exactly what I wanted to know" (182). Finally, she gives in to that impulse, and extracts Judith's story.

With some justice, Joan Myers Weimer describes this as a "predatory narrator" with "a compulsive fascination with solitude perhaps greater than her own, as well as a need to feel someone else's pain" (6). Or, as Ann Douglas Wood puts it, this is a narrator who acts upon "her almost uncontrollable need to get at the other woman's story—which she finally elicits—and by so doing, to get at some stifled part of herself" (130). Woolson shows us how the narrator's desire to understand Judith serves her own emotional needs.

Woolson also asks us to question the particular terms of this narrator's understanding. Through their dialogues, the narrator comes to understand Judith Kinsolving as a casualty of the Civil War, every aspect of her condition—her poverty, isolation, pessimism, resentfulness—explained by the atrocities of the war, which left her father and two brothers dead, her husband shot as a spy, and her lands ravaged. Judith has become a sentimental victim:

> Torpidly I draw my breath through day and night, nor care if the rain falls or the sun shines. . . . I live on as the palsied animal lives, and if some day the spring fails, and the few herbs within [her nephew's] reach, he dies. Nor do I think he grieves much about it; he only eats from habit. So do I. (187)

At this point, the frame-narrator can fully "understand" Judith by placing her in a script of national catharsis, a script which renders Judith useful. By absorbing Judith into a victim-and-benefactor drama, the narrator metonymically appropriates the South to a characteristically Northern historical narrative. She illustrates what Amy Kaplan describes as a general Reconstruction-era revision of the Civil War, "which writers and politicians actively 'forgot' as mutual slaughter and rewrote as a shared sacrifice for reunion" (242). Judith is made to fit this script, made to confirm the narrator's self-image, categories of thought, and frame of reference. Understanding here serves a possessive impulse.

In pointing out the invasive and possessive aspects of the anthropological impulse, I am not revealing anything that these authors are not aware of. Indeed, there is a whole body of local colour fiction devoted to exposing and criticizing the worst of the anthropological posture. Charles Egbert Craddock's "The Star in the Valley" is a classic example. The protagonist, Reginald Chevis, is a city-man hunting in the Cumberland mountains. He casts himself as an amateur anthropologist, "always on the alert to add to his stock of knowledge of men and minds, always analyzing his own inner life and the inner life of those about him" (140-41). As Craddock writes, "he piqued himself on the readiness with which he became interested in these people, entered into their thoughts and feelings, [and] obtained a comprehensive idea of the machinery of life in this wilderness" (134). But "Star in the Valley" denies and ironizes Chevis's claims. While Chevis thinks his worldliness and cultivation enable him to appreciate the mountaineers, these qualities ultimately lead him to a romanticized view which prohibits any genuine understanding. Chevis felt that the mountaineers "appealed to him from the basis of their common humanity" (143) and that "he entertained a broader view" of them than most, but "he had not even a subacute idea that he looked upon these people and their inner life only as picturesque bits of the mental and moral landscape; that it was an aesthetic and theoretical pleasure their contemplation offered him; that he was as far as ever from the basis of common humanity" (135). By the end of the story, Chevis is forced to recognize

> that despite all his culture, his sensibility, his yearnings toward humanity, he was not so high a thing in the scale of being; that he had placed a false estimate upon himself. He had looked down upon [Celia] with a mingled pity for her dense ignorance, her coarse surroundings, her low station, and a dilettante's delight at picturesque effects, and with no recognition of the moral splendors of that star in the valley. (152)

This story, and a number of others like it,[6] offers a limited critique, acknowledging the problems with the anthropological stance toward regional life. Even more trenchant are those works that reveal and explore radically different aspects of regionalism's ethnographic dimension. One such possibility is that the regional cultures under scrutiny here are subjects as well as objects—that this "material" can have some agency, some influence on the observer.

This possibility lurks in the margins of Woolson's "Cotton Country." Surely the narrator extorts Judith Kinsolving's story and appropriates it to her own ends. But, at the same time, Judith is playing her interlocutor like a violin. She delights in challenging her listener. Then Judith affirms that her husband was shot as a spy: "You start—you question—you doubt. But spies were shot in those days, were they not?" (189). Later: "You did not expect such an ending, did you?" (190). Still later: "Bitter, am I? Put yourself in my place" (195). And she casts herself as the sentimental victim only after getting to know the frame-narrator and determining that this will be the way to gain her sympathy and material aid. Each character in this story is exploiting the other.

Even more cogent are those works that imply that the observer, by getting to know an alien culture, is changed. If understanding means "getting inside" and simply "getting," it also means being "taken in."

This phenomenon takes a positive face in Joel Chandler Harris's "Azalia." This story juxtaposes two observers, Boston women come to the South during Reconstruction. Harriet Tewksbury embodies an appropriative mode of understanding, absorbing what she sees to her Yankee paradigms of Industry and Progress. Meanwhile, Helen Eustis, her niece, embodies an alternative form of understanding. Helen demonstrates that the "understanding" that comes from her anthropological investigation challenges and alters the self more than the material she observes. She says, "I have been trying to pretend to myself, ever since we left Washington, that we are traveling through a strange country; but it is a mere pretense. I have been trying to verify some previous impressions of barbarism and shiftlessness. . . . I have been trying to take the newspaper view . . . but it is impossible. We must correct the newspapers, Aunt Harriet" (211). Harriet fits the South to her prior notions. Helen, fitting her concepts to what she observes and experiences, models an accommodating rather than appropriative form of knowledge. Helen allows herself to be challenged by the South's otherness, and alters herself to fit it.

An anthropologist would say that Helen has "gone native." If this is beneficial, it is also threatening, at least in anthropology's traditional way of thinking—threatening because it pits the impulse to submit to one's material against the need to preserve one's objectivity and integrity. George Washington Cable's novel *The Grandissimes* offers an unusually thorough exposition of this struggle. Joseph Frowenfeld, a Yankee apothecary, finds himself thrown into New Orleans just after the Louisiana Purchase of 1804. He initially finds the Creole world totally baffling. But as he develops personal attachments, he becomes an anthropological figure, embarking on an effort to interpret what Cable calls "this newly found book, the Community of New Orleans" (131).

Like Jewett's protagonist in *Deephaven*, Frowenfeld embarks upon a project of "reading" the culture around him. But while Helen finds her surroundings transparent, Frowenfeld finds his unintelligible. Cable fills *The Grandissimes* with episodes of masking, secrecy, and riddles, all of which constitute impediments to knowledge. The challenge begins when Frowenfeld's physician tells him about a past quadroon ball. The anecdote

> was little more than a thick mist of strange names, places and events; yet there shone a light of romance upon it that filled it with colour and populated it with phantoms. Frowenfeld's interest rose—was allured into this mist—and there was left befogged. . . . In the midst of the mist Frowenfeld encountered and grappled with a problem of human life in Creole type, the possible correlations of whose quantities we shall presently find him revolving in a studious and sympathetic mind. (20)

All this threatens to overwhelm the observer. Frowenfeld "was brain-weary. Even in the bright recollection of the lady and her talk he became involved among shadows, and going from bad to worse, seemed at length almost to gasp in an atmosphere of hints, allusions, faint unspoken admissions, ill-concealed antipathies, unfinished speeches, mistaken identities and whisperings of hidden strife" (122).

Because "this newly found book, the Community of New Orleans" is so difficult, Frowenfeld cannot read it properly until he learns to see things from a more Creole point of view. Understanding requires assimilation. To obtain a genuine cultural knowledge, the novel implies, the observer must adapt to his material. This is the promise that *The Grandissimes*, like "Azalia," holds out for anthropological thought.

It is also the danger. As Frowenfeld assimilates he gains knowledge of one type, but also loses the objective distance which gives his understanding value. Frowenfeld's apartness initially alienates him from the society he wants to influence, but it also establishes his authority. As Frowenfeld's Creole friend explains, insiders have a weaker claim to knowledge than outsiders: "we are judged from a distance. We forget that we ourselves are too close to see distinctly, and so continue, a spectacle to civilization, sitting in a horrible darkness" (200). Moreover, an adaptive understanding carries a personal risk: true assimilation means losing oneself in the culture one observes. Through Frowenfeld, Cable explores the threat of "going native." The Creole friend counsels Frowenfeld, "You must get acclimated . . . not in body only, that you have done; but in mind—in taste—in conversation—and in convictions too" (46). "The water," he argues, "must expect to take the shape of the bucket" (46). Frowenfeld at first objects, "One need not be water!" (47). But along with epiphany comes personal threat:

> As quietly as a spider [Frowenfeld] was spinning information into knowledge and knowledge into what is supposed to be wisdom; whether it was or not we shall see. His unidentified merchant friend who had adjured him to become acclimated as 'they all did' had also exhorted him to study the human mass of which he had become a unit; but whether that study, if pursued, was sweetening and ripening, or whether it was corrupting him, that friend did not come to see. (76)

Cable's novel, in short, dramatizes a simple enthymeme: understanding requires assimilation, and assimilation amounts to a loss of one's self in one's material. *The Grandissimes* inverts the argument of "In the Cotton Country," where understanding amounts to appropriation of one's material. The result is possession *by* rather than possession *of*. This is both the promise and the threat of cultural knowledge.

Exposing this promise and threat in their ethnographic subplots, Cable and his contemporaries anticipate recent debates in anthropology with remarkable precision. According to many writers, anthropological knowledge operates primarily as an agent of dominance. By turning other cultures into objects of knowledge, ethnography subordinates or appropriates them to a ruling order's frames of reference. As Edward Said writes, "Knowledge means rising above immediacy, beyond self, into the foreign and distant. The object of such knowledge is inherently vulnerable to scrutiny. . . . To have such knowledge of a thing is to dominate it, to have authority over it" (32).

Others point out that ethnography can serve distinctly contrary ends. "Although anthropology does to some degree make an object of the 'other,'" P. Steven Sangren writes, it also takes a comparative, relativistic approach which invites challenge to the observer's dominance. "The discipline was dialogic long before the term was popular," Sangren argues; a "comparative study of ideology," it "makes insights like Said's possible" in the first place (406). In a similar vein, Vincent Crapanzano argues that

> the anthropologist has to listen to those whom he studies; he has constantly to relativize his own position, to question his most basic assumptions about himself and the nature of the world in which he lives and to contemplate, with requisite courage and irony too, the always somewhat terrifying possibility of otherness. In other words, inherent in the ethnographic stance is a subversion of that stance. The anthropologist is always at risk. (139)

Cultural knowledge can operate as both a power grab and as a self critique. The local colourists figured this out long before ambiguity and self-consciousness became fashionable in anthropology. They bequeath to us, "regionalists" of a century later, a curiously ambivalent lesson: that "understanding" offers a bridge across cultural divides, but a perilous one.

Notes

1. For a snapshot of this debate, see P. Steven Sangren's "Rhetoric and the Authority of Ethnography" and the rejoinders which follow it.

2. For variations on this distinction see Robert Penn Warren's "Not Local Color," James D Hart's "Regionalism," and Marjorie Pryse's "Reading Regionalism."

3. Without fully developing the implications, other critics have noted the ethnographic qualities of this literature. Eric J. Sundquist, for example, notes in it "an anthropological dimension in which new 'regions' are opened to fictional or journalistic exploration and analysis" (503); Amy Kaplan similarly observes that "like the subjects of anthropological fieldwork (developing as a scientific discipline in this period), native inhabitants [of literary 'regions'] possessed primitive qualities that made them worthy of study also and left them in need to interpretation by outsiders" (252).

4. Compare, for example, John Wesley Powell's *Introduction to the Study of Indian Language* (which classifies aboriginal languages by vocabulary), and the 1892 "Library Edition" of Edward Eggleston's *The Hoosier Schoolmaster* (with its copious etymological footnotes on Hoosier diction) — or, for that matter, the polyphonic fiction of Kate Chopin and George Washington Cable.

5. As a general rule, of course, American anthropology focused on the cultures of non-white peoples and local colour on the cultures of white people. But even this distinction grows fuzzy in the work of Charles Chesnutt, Helen Hunt Jackson, and Kate Chopin, among others.

6. See, for example, Hamlin Garland's "God's Ravens," Jewett's "A White Heron," Kate Chopin's "The Gentleman of Bayou T'che," and Alice Dunbar-Nelson's "M'sieu Fortier's Violin," the last three of which receive insightful discussion in Majorie Pryse's "Reading Regionalism."

ALISON CALDER   University of Western Ontario

Reassessing Prairie Realism

PRAIRIE WRITING IS A CLICHÉ: gophers and grain elevators erect themselves against an oppressive sky. Dwarfed by natural forces, a man battles his way through a blizzard and someone lights a lamp at noon. Though such writing relates mainly to a relatively short historical period and to a relatively small geographic area, and though the cultural conditions that led to its literary production have changed drastically in the last fifty years, examples of prairie realism have continued to dominate fiction canons in Canadian academia. Dick Harrison remarks in *Unnamed Country* that "both [the promise and the threat inherent in settling the prairie] are reflected in the mass of popular fiction, but we generally accept the development of prairie realism, with its preference for the stark and threatening aspect of the plains as the culmination of prairie fiction" (xi). Neither Harrison nor critics writing after him go on to raise the questions such a statement demands: why is prairie realism so widely accepted as the pinnacle of prairie fiction? Who is the "we" of whom Harrison writes? What significance should be granted to the fact that the prairies are continually being reportrayed in the classroom as hostile, life-denying, and imaginatively sterile? What does it mean that we usually read and teach only a literature that places the prairies solely in the context of the past? And what happens to the writers of the last fifty years whose works do not fit into a "realistic" and therefore tragic view of prairie existence?

In this paper I will offer some suggestions about the implications of the way prairie realist fiction is taught, as well as the effects of that teaching. The term prairie realism, as I use it, refers to works like Sinclair Ross's *As For Me and My House*, F.P. Grove's *Settlers on the Marsh*, Martha

Ostenso's *Wild Geese,* and Robert Stead's *Grain.*¹ Each of these is frequently described as "a classic of prairie realism"; rarely is one described as "a Canadian classic." There is a significant difference here, between "prairie" and "Canadian," and that difference points to one of the difficulties encountered in dealing with prairie realism. Prairie realism is, by definition, regional; it is *prairie* literature. When it comes under the label of "regional," as it frequently does in the classroom, it is perceived in a specific way. Regional literature, at least in Canada, is defined as being both realistic and referential. Its value resides in its ability to mirror a specific environment, to show what real "life" is like in, as Edward McCourt says, "a limited and peculiar environment" (55).

The purpose of such literature is then in some senses pedagogical. E. K. Brown accentuates this aspect of regionalism, writing that, at their best, such writings "clarify for the reader his own nature and those of his associates" (18). A similar impetus underlies Northrop Frye's later assessment of the function of Canadian literature in general; he writes of what he perceives as the Canadian public's "obvious and unquenchable desire . . . to identify itself through its literature" (823). However, such writings not only reflect a nation or region, but also create it. By clarifying his or her nature to the reader, by saying "this is what you are," the books in effect teach the reader what it is to be a prairie dweller or a northerner—in short, these works both define regional characteristics and establish a set of criteria for evaluating their presence.² Such definition is necessary, Brown contends, because of the ignorance Canadians have about their country, and their lack of desire to learn about it: he writes, in a provocative statement, that "there is little eagerness to explore the varieties of Canadian life, little awareness how much variety exists, or what a peril that variety is, in time of crisis, to national unity" (23). Brown's assertion displays an interesting doubleness: Canadians must learn of the extent of their diversity in order to suppress it.

While Brown sees regionalism as valuable in a documentary sense, he ultimately rejects it as an important form of expression. His assessment is worth quoting at length:

> Regionalist art may be expected to possess certain virtues. One of these is accuracy, not merely of fact, but accuracy of tone; and throughout our literature there has been a disposition to force the note, to make life appear nobler or gayer or more intense than life

really is in its typical expressions. It would help us towards cultural maturity if we had a set of novels, or sketches, or memoirs, that described the life of Canadian towns and cities as it really is, works in which nothing would be presented that the author had not encountered in his own experience. . . . In the end, however, regionalist art will fail because it stresses the superficial and peculiar at the expense, at least, if not to the exclusion, of the fundamental and universal. The advent of regionalism may be welcomed with reservations as a stage through which it may be well for us to pass, as a discipline and a purgation. (23-24)

Regionalism appears here to be a national castor oil. There are a number of things in Brown's assessment to keep in mind when considering the ways in which the definitions of regionalism in general, and prairie realism in particular, work. Brown's vision of regionalism is resolutely realistic in style, presenting regional life "as it really is" and being concerned, above all, with accurate reportage. The regional writer, denied the use of his or her imagination, can only reveal the precise events of his or her own milieu; nothing must be included that "the author had not encountered in his own experience." However, the emphasis Brown places on actual life experience, on telling it like it is, is troubled by his assessment that Canadian writers have tended to "force the note" and to intensify that life experience. Since all life experience is necessarily subjective—it is, after all, *your* life—Brown's assessment of reality's tone appears as a legislation of the ways in which reality is represented, a control on the way in which regional writers articulate their own experiences. While it is important to Brown that a record of "real life" in the provinces exists, in order for that record to be valid it must match Brown's own perceptions.

Key also to Brown's definition of regionalism is the idea of regression. Regionalism is a stage, like childhood, through which we must pass in order to achieve "maturity." It may be a tool to help us achieve a mature art, but it can never itself be mature. (I would like to point out that Brown's hierarchization of "regional" literature vs. "real" Canadian literature is continually re-enacted through the insertion of regionally based texts into a national curriculum only under the rubric of the regional.) This immaturity is built into the very definition of regionalism—it will fail because it must focus on what Brown perceives as the limited, enclosed region, rather than attempting to treat "fundamental and universal" values. Should it attempt such treatment, it can no longer be considered regional: the definition of the genre has a built-in obsolescence. Regional works are then, by their nature, doomed. They must always be nostalgic, must always look backwards, providing an unchanging picture of life as it *was*, rather than as it is or might be.

So regional writing lives a curious double life. On the one hand, it must convey the individual and the particular. On the other hand, it must be homogenizing, reporting on the general life of the region, smoothing over any internal conflicts to present a unified view of life "in its typical expressions." There is no point, after all, in regional writing if it takes apart the region it is supposed to be creating; Brown's definition of regionalism cannot support such a dispersal. This homogenizing process extends beyond the region under scrutiny as well, as the value of regional writing is seen to reside not in what the text says about the region, but in what it says about the centre.[3] The value of the regional text lies in what it indirectly implies about "universal truths"—in other words, what *your* story says about *me*. Because of this insistence on "universal truths," whose presence distinguishes a "regional" text from one that is merely "local colour"—and the distinction between these is entirely another matter—the region, in this model of regionalism, is always necessarily defined by those who are external to it. The region has value, or is defined by, what in it is analogous to something in the centre. If there is no correspondence between the way in which the region is represented and the way the centre perceives itself, then the text fails as a regional entity, becoming simply "bad writing." This centre/region correspondence can be based on similarity—family values can be affirmed, for example—or on difference, where the region exists for the centre to define itself against—you are country, I am city; you are quaint, I am sophisticated.

I have taken the time to run over some of the dominant characteristics of the most common model of regional literature. There are other, more recent and to me more interesting definitions of regionalism—as a resistance movement, for example. But when it comes to prairie realism, text, critic, and reader are all fixed in the past. Prairie realism, as such, is no longer being written. Contemporary prairie writers are exploring new content, like the urban prairie; new forms, like post-modernism and magic realism; and new genres, like the detective story. But with the exception of an author like Robert Kroetsch, such writers are rarely taught in Canadian Literature courses, except in a more specialized context, as in a course on

Western Canadian writing, or prairie women writers.[4] The question then remains—what is so compelling about prairie realism? Why is it continually being taught? There are several obvious answers: these are texts that teachers have themselves been taught; inexpensive editions are relatively easy to find; and they are easy to peg into that blank space on the course syllabus marked "regional text."[5] But if these texts are continually taught as representative regional texts, and, as regional texts, they exist as representations of the real life of a region, exactly what sort of a region is being represented?

This question is a little more complex than it might appear. It is fairly easy to enumerate the qualities of the prairies as they appear in prairie regional fiction. The land and climate are everything. The prairies exist in a permanent, drought-produced dust storm, the tedium of which is broken only by the occasional blizzard. It is always circa 1935. There are no colours and no animals, unless you count domestic livestock that freeze or smother. Human beings die natural deaths only in that their deaths are caused by nature: they freeze, suffocate, drown, burn, or are driven to suicide. There are no urban centres; the ones that do exist are immeasurably far away from the isolated farm houses where the works are set. Even when there is a town, no one speaks to another; no one has any friends. There are vicious rivalries but no politics. Sex, when it occurs, is frequently adulterous, and usually followed by death.

All of this is not to trivialize the stories themselves, which contain considerably more of interest than such a sketch allows. Pieces like Ross's "The Painted Door" and Grove's "Snow" are important prairie writings that depict the destructive impact of the conditions of prairie life on people existing under a certain set of conditions at a certain point in time. However, the majority of critical articles written about these and other works of prairie realism fail to recognize both that these writings present fictionalized, not photographic, landscapes, and that the empirical conditions of life represented in those fictions no longer necessarily exist. Narrow definitions of regionalism that follow after Brown's contribute to these misrepresentations: if a novel is regional, which is what we are told prairie realism is, then it *must*, by definition, be "true." The fiction cannot be fiction: it must be representative of a typical regional ethos. And if it is going to present something "true," then it must present something which is fixed and universal. To admit regional change is to admit the possibility of change in general—if a region is going to function as a microcosm of the centre, as it must in this critical economy, then any flux in the region threatens the stability of the macrocosm.

Criticism of prairie realism is predicated on a belief in the primacy of the land. Geographic determinism is evident even in the critical label: this is, after all, *prairie* realism. This label provides more than just geographic demarcation, however, in that assumption of geographic authority carries illusions of immutability and homogeneity. Such illusions are a critical necessity. In order for the category "prairie realism" to exist, there must be similarities between the works considered. In this case, the most obvious similarity is setting, which becomes the common denominator and so the defining characteristic of the school. This definition has not changed since Edward McCourt described the prairie writer in 1949. The writer

> must be a pictorial artist able to describe accurately the physical features of the prairie landscape; he should be a poet with the power to feel and to re-create imaginatively the particular atmosphere which invests the prairie scene; and lastly, he should be a psychologist with sufficient knowledge of human nature to be able to understand and describe the influence of the region on the people who live within its confines. (55)

McCourt's prairie writer appears as a type of documentary geographer, producing case studies of the effect of prairie life on the average individual. Like Brown, McCourt grounds his definition of regional writing in attention to local detail: the writer must "describe accurately" the regional environment. But while a dependency on geography may seem innocuous enough, environmental determinism is far from neutral. As Francesco Loriggio points out,

> when we label a novel 'Southern fiction,' or, in Canada, 'Prairie fiction,' we are implying that no matter how much the characters are spurred on by private or personal motivation, their behavior will be seen as a function of their relation with the place in which they live. (14)

As a result, the actions of the characters, and indeed the construction of the characters themselves, is seen as a result of environmental determinism, or, in McCourt's phrase, because of "the influence of the region on the people who live within its confines."[6] Stories unfold the way they do because such an unfolding, given the environment, is inevitable. This sense of inevitability confers the truth-value of regionalism on works designated as prairie realist fiction. Such truth-value turns on the idea of a regional homogeneity which is at best arbitrary and artificial. Gerald Haslam points out the problem of critically constructing a regional writing: "We are faced with a semantic dilemma: we say *West*, and consequently search for common characteristics, when in fact we must deal with *Wests*" (4). Predicating a critical economy on the idea of environmental determinism stabilizes the multiple meanings of "prairie" through erasure of the region's many internal conflicts, as attention to landscape precludes consideration of gender, race, and class conflicts included (or suppressed) in these texts. This effacement permits the region to be constructed as a seamless microcosm, in which any troubles are both regionally produced and regionally contained.

Differences in the prairie landscape, and the different responses to it, are similarly effaced. The relation of human to environment in prairie realist fiction is resoundingly negative. The land is seen, in some cases, as a malevolent force; just as often it is depicted as merely uncaring as it wipes out the unwary settler. But this struggle to populate the land is also taken to another critical level where the real battle is seen not as one between settler and landscape, but between *writer* and landscape. The belief in such an adversarial relationship is evident even in the titles of the two most influential book-length studies of prairie literature: Dick Harrison's *Unnamed Country: The Struggle for a Canadian Prairie Fiction*, and Laurie Ricou's *Vertical Man, Horizontal World*. Harrison makes the nature of that struggle clear, writing that it is "the encounter between the civilized imagination and an unnamed landscape" (xii) that is at the crux of all prairie writing. This civilized mind/uncivilized country confrontation is a commonplace in Canadian criticism—Robert Kroetsch's question "How do you write in a new country?" is a concern that can be traced from the first writers in Canada. This discussion is frequently cast in terms of authenticity and artifice: we praise those Canadian authors who find aesthetic forms that are "natural" to Canada, and condemn those who got by with imported forms.[7] But for some reason the prairie is thought of as particularly hard to civilize and articulate, and is continually cast as the hinterland to a central Canadian baseland. Harrison, for example, asserts that the prairie is "particularly intractable to the imagination" (xiii), while Robert Thacker writes in *The Great Prairie Fact and Literary Imagination* that while nineteenth-century literature is generally marked by a tension between romance and realism, in prairie fiction "that tension was exacerbated by the nature of the landscape itself, forcing the demands of prairie space into literary consciousness" (104). Exactly why the prairie should be any more intractable than the forest or the mountain or the valley is unclear, but at any rate critics endow the encounter of the individual with the prairie landscape with special significance. The nature of that encounter is predetermined, however: writing about W.O. Mitchell's *Who Has Seen the Wind*, Harrison remarks that "it is obviously somewhere in the 'realist' tradition, *yet* it emphasizes the positive response to the unknown country" (xi, italics mine). Similarly, he asserts that *As For Me and My House* is seen as the premiere work of prairie realism because its narrator, Mrs. Bentley, "expresses so well the reactive, defensive function of the imagination confronting the prairie" (xi). Here we see the critical homogenization of the regional at work. Mrs. Bentley's response is generalized to that of "the imagination," and Ross's depiction of her extreme response is normalized and seen as somehow natural to the landscape. There is little awareness displayed of the historical specificity of such a response; the imagination will always confront the prairie in exactly the same way. To maintain such a belief requires a certain blindness to empirical reality—Harrison goes on to remark that people respond to the prairies in the same way because "the austere face of the prairie has not changed that much since Henry Kelsey first saw it," and that "the incongruities of that first response to the plains have never been overcome" (28). Such an assessment is only possible when one responds to a prairie that is utterly immutable and timeless, a prairie that exists only in fiction.

Likewise, Ricou addresses what he perceives as the fundamental problem confronting every prairie writer: how to "interpret a landscape that is without sounds and devoid of anything concrete to catch the eye and stimulate the imagination" (76). Such a statement is, of course, both extreme and ridiculous; at the same time that Ricou discusses the inarticulate characters portrayed in prairie realist fiction, he ignores the actual artistic products, the books, that those characters inhabit. The belief in the "reality" the stories depict overshadows the existence of the stories themselves. Again, we see the idea that prairie realism is not fiction but a reflection of a harsh reality; because the prairie is largely presented in these works as a sealed, lifeless, and inevitably doomed region, that is what, to critics, it becomes.[8] The prairie that the prairie realists construct becomes real for these critics, and that constructed prairie is then used as a standard of evaluation to measure other books. Ricou is led to make statements like, "In attempting to depict the universal meaninglessness posited by existentialism the western Canadian writer found an obvious metaphor in the prairie landscape" (148), and Harrison praises an early prairie author for his authentic presentation of prairie life, writing that "his narrative of a death in a blizzard . . . is one of the best before F.P. Grove" (59).

Lest I seem to be picking on easy targets, since both Harrison's and Ricou's books came out twenty years ago, I should point out that they have remained widely influential. Their conceptions of the prairie turn up again and again, most recently in David Jordan's *New World Regionalism*, which came out in 1994. Jordan's analysis of Kroetsch's *Gone Indian* still relates directly to his perception of the landscape itself, rather than to its artistic representation. He writes that "all [flying scenes in *Gone Indian*] are tied to the inherent need of the region's inhabitants to break free of the horizontal monotony of the prairie landscape" (113), and follows that up with the assessment that "the predominant reaction to the prairie environment that *Gone Indian* describes is the need to find or build a vertical structure that breaks the horizontal monotony of the prairie environment" (114). Here we have the double curse—not only is the entire prairie experience compressed into an essentializing horizontal/vertical model, but the empirical landscape itself is tossed off as being "monotonous." The prairie is still seen as "devoid of anything concrete to catch the eye and stimulate the imagination." I suggest that the belief that the prairie is *only* a wasted earth and burning sun, that there is *no* imaginative possibility here, creates a critical environment in which prairie realism, with its matter-of-fact style, is seen to be a "natural" mode of representing the prairie, and is therefore granted a privileged position in a canon which itself privileges mimesis.

That prairie realism is still critically invested with truth-value is demonstrated in comments like these of Thacker: "Philip's art, Mrs. Bentley asserts, is in a certain sense a transcription of the prairie landscape—Stouck has called it a mirror—and so is Sinclair Ross's and all those [prairie realists] treated here" (205). The perceived transparency of prairie realist fiction could not be clearer: as a hostile prairie environment reflected in a documentary mirror. These critical responses are symbiotic; the reinforcement of prairie realism and the representational values it implies supports the negative view of the prairie, which, in turn, increases the status of these works. At the same time, both prairie realism and the real prairies are contained: prairie realist works are slotted into the "regional text" place with all its attendant evaluative baggage, and the real prairies are continually defined as a sparsely populated, inarticulate, sterile region, whose lack of power and/or wealth is no one's fault but its own.

Such a construction has real consequence. As Gerald Haslam points out, "Archibald MacLeish has called the West 'a country in the mind,' a compelling definition except that the West is also a real place or series of places, inhabited by real people"(2). If the prairies are continually being reified as an area which is unlivable, which is a permanent Palliser's Triangle, then the political forces that have been to an extent responsible for the continuing exploitation of that region are absolved of any responsibility for the region's decline. Like the failure of the Maritime fishing industry, the failure of the prairies' agriculturally-based economies is seen as the fault of the people who live there. Since the region is clearly unlivable, to attempt to pursue a life there seems laughable at best. I am not suggesting that prairie realism is to blame. But I am suggesting that when we, as academics, teach works which we consider to be regional, we had better examine very carefully our presuppositions, our underlying definitions of regionalism and region—our own and those of other critics that we cite. At a time when we are being told that place and referentiality no longer matter, that there is no national literature, and that we are living in a world without boundaries, those of us who call the have-not political regions home are becoming aware that placing ourselves, and our literatures, is more important than ever.

Notes

1. It should be noted that there are considerable differences in the types of realism texts employ.
2. Prairie dwellers must display certain qualifications; for example, hard-working, plain-speaking, slow-talking.
3. I refer here to the metropolitan centres of Canada. These centres are, of course, regions themselves, though they frequently avoid that label.
4. The extent of Kroetsch's critical writings contributes to his anomalous position.
5. Ernest Buckler's *The Mountain and the Valley* is another perennial winner of this title.
6. McCourt's use of the word "confines" suggests the limitation and evaluation embedded in this regional definition .
7. It bears repeating that no aesthetic forms are natural.
8. A number of other cultural and political factors work towards such a definition of region; to deal with them adequately is beyond the scope of this paper.

West of "Woman," Or, Where No Man Has Gone Before

Geofeminism in Aritha Van Herk

ACCORDING TO CATHY N. DAVIDSON, in an essay published in the 1985 collection *Regionalism and the Female Imagination*, for the female characters in the fiction of Margaret Laurence "geography is close to destiny" (Davidson 129); the phrase returns without the qualifying modality in Carol Shields's 1992 novel *The Republic of Love*: "Geography is destiny, says Fay's good friend Iris Jaffe, and Fay tends to agree" (78). While her wording is different, Aritha Van Herk shows herself to be fully aware of the relation between geography and destiny in her 1990 novel (or "geografictione") *Places Far From Ellesmere*: "How to find yourself: see map" (71). Thus Van Herk's work appears to share a more general preoccupation of modern Canadian women writers with the question of regionalism and regional writing that is no longer simply concerned with "local colour," but with an investigation into the coordinates of female identity and imagination. Recognizing, that is, the complex interrelatedness of geography and psychology, and geography and power, Van Herk has produced a series of novels in which the female protagonists continually try, to adapt one of her own phrases, to re/invent themselves past the boundaries of their destined regions—the home, the family, the domestic, and, particularly, conventional male constructions of Woman.[1]

Identifying herself as a "political feminist" (Jones 6), Van Herk's concerns with regionalism have centred on what Teresa de Lauretis has described as "the conditions of representability of another social subject" (Aesthetic 182). Ever since the publication, in 1978, of her prize-winning first novel *Judith*, Aritha Van Herk has been preoccupied with the "re/un/ reading" of her personal geography. She has done so from an awareness of being doubly regionalized: her place on the map of Canadian literature is determined by the coordinates of gender and geographical provenance. Avoiding the negative denotation of "marginalization," Van Herk has tried to realign her quest for self-realization and self-creation with the trinity of "race, class, and gender" by privileging—often in provocative ways—the "other" or "absent" categories of the (Canadian) "west" and "woman" as part of what might be termed a feminist ideology of regionalism, or "geofeminism": "Certainly the fictive act of landscape has influenced me, as has the fact that I belong to the region of woman. That sense of otherness, which is one of the strongest elements of regionalism, is what I work with—an effort to define the otherness that others have so far ignored" (Jones 1).

A child of Dutch immigrant parents, Van Herk grew up on a farm near the village of Edberg, in central Alberta, a region she returns to in many of her writings. Canada's western prairie in Van Herk's work is more, however, than a mere physical space or landscape—the regional, the rural, the not-east, or the not-Toronto. "Region," Van Herk once stated, "is that which defines the artist.... I take the perspective of my particular region: my place, the west; my background, first-generation child of immigrant parents; my sex, a woman; my form, fiction; and finally, my work, a writer" (Frozen 79). The "west" is for Van Herk a significant beyond which includes "not only time, place, and space, but also sexuality, religion, and politics, aspects of a person's life that ... validate region" (Jones 1). Essentially, the "west" is therefore a psychic condition, a state of being independent of the coordinates of time and place—of textually represented time and place. That is, "region is not only a place where you live but it is a specific way of looking at the world, particularly a specific way of looking at literature and writing so that it reflects what *you* think is textual" (Jones 1). However, for Van Herk, being in many ways a child of the age of poststructuralism, the limitations of linguistic discourse are not so much problematic as an unavoidable parameter of all writing. Van Herk's main quarrel with the conventional, pre-geofeminist discourse of regionalism is not merely with its inadequacy as a representative medium, but with the fact that it *represents*: the fact that language is by necessity ideologically charged with cultural codes and value systems, which—and this is the crux—are not necessarily hers, or woman's.

Of course these ideological and cultural codes of national myth have traditionally nowhere been reflected more explicitly than in the North American cultural concept of the west, or, more accurately, in the way the west has traditionally been represented in the east: that is, as a place dominated by the contingencies of survival, privileging those biological, social and psychic characteristics commonly associated with the male gender, such as physical strength, hardihood, inventiveness, determination, and rationality. By setting herself up as a prairie feminist writer and appropriating the myth of the west in her work, Van Herk consciously tries to unwrite the conventional value systems that lie embedded in that myth. She not only wants to go beyond the language of the west as such, but also beyond conventional representations of woman, by first colonizing and deconstructing the heavily encoded male discourse of the myth of the west, and then reinscribing a subversively recoined version back into the original myth: "That regional prerogative needs to be cracked wide open. By stretching the borders of the region we inhabit as women, we are inducing hair-line cracks, fissures, in all the things that men have defined as their territory, or the larger world" (Jones 3).

This raises the question of whether geofeminist literature should be realistic and representational. "Women," Van Herk stated in the 1987 interview, "can write kitchen-sink realism about the limitations of their lives forever. But realism can become its own prison, its own enclosure. Fiction's mandate is to explore the possibilities of the imagination, the possibilities of the world beyond its closure" (Jones 7). Van Herk's attempt "to escape the page, to escape ink and [her] own implacable literacy" reaches its fullest expression so far in *In Visible Ink*, a collection of essays published in 1991 (4). In the title-piece of that collection Van Herk offers the personal narrative of a trip to Canada's frozen and snow-covered arctic as a trope for an exploration of the realm beyond language:

> I am simply here, reduced to *being*, breathing the ice-crystal air through my nose and into my lungs, stamping my feet against the granular snow to revive my circulation. I am at last beyond language, at last literately invisible.
>
> Which is, reader, I confess, the state I ideally wish to attain. Finally, finally, in a life dominated by language, I am to some degree

free of it, of having to speak and read and write. If you have read *Places Far From Ellesmere*, you know that the time I spent at Lake Hazen in the northern part of Ellesmere Island taught me unreading, the act of dismantling a text past all its previous readings and writings. The landscape there, its delicious remoteness, calm unmeasurability, catalyzed my reading act into something beyond reading, enabling me to untie all the neatly laced up expectations of words and their printing, their arrangement on the page, the pages bound together into a directive narrative, that then refused to be static, but turned and began to read back, to read me, to unread my very reading and my personal geography. (3-4)

The central theme in Van Herk's work, then, is the re-writing of the west as a means to re/write the self, her woman's self. Van Herk's writing is not only an attempt to go beyond the boundaries of conventional fiction, to go "west of fiction" (to use the title of a collection of short stories which she coedited with Leah Flater and Rudy Wiebe for NeWest Press), but also an attempt to escape from the confines of conventional womanhood as represented in a male-dominated discourse of the west and in history and writing in general: to go west of woman, so to speak.

The question I wish to pursue in this essay, however, is not so much *how* Van Herk tries to go beyond the exclusionary realm of masculinist discourse, but whether she succeeds in her ambition to represent imaginatively her "invisible and unlanguaged self" through the medium and mediation of narrative fiction (*In Visible* 10). To put it differently, I will attempt to assess to what extent Van Herk manages to, as she once described it, "de-sire the language"—to overcome, in other words, "the linguistic bias that the particularities of male experience are considered to be universal while those of female experience are too trivial to merit expression" (*In Visible* 81). To be sure, the task Van Herk has set herself—to restore "desire" (that is, both the source of artistic creation and the urge for self-expression) to "realism" and to the language in which it is mediated—is a formidable one, seeing that the challenge she is facing is not merely artistic and ideological, but an epistemological one as well: the fact, namely, that "Language acts both as jailor and liberator; its very usage restricts, yet nothing is acknowledged to exist without it.... After all, it is desire which brings about the need for words, the urge to give utterance to the deepest of human feelings. And yet, without the language to name it, desire could not be" (*Frozen* 81; 84). In the following, however, I will argue that while casting off the fetters of realism and crossing the conventional generic boundaries that separate the imaginative and the cognitive, the metaphorical and the argumentative, Van Herk may have succeeded in reformulating a daunting epistemological question in increasingly provocative terms, but that she did so only at the expense of her own artistic and creative aspirations: in other words, that she has sacrificed "language" to "desire."

Although most extensively explored in the experimental "geografictione" *Places Far From Ellesmere*, Van Herk's preoccupation with the problematic relation between a hegemonic masculinist discourse and the region of her female identity can be traced back to her earlier, more conventional fictional writings. The first of these is Van Herk's debut novel, *Judith*. It tells the story of Judith, an only child, who grows up on a pig farm outside the town of Norberg, opts for a life in the city when she is in her late teens, and who, being disillusioned with city-life, returns to the country, where, like her father before her, she now runs a pig farm — a self-conscious act of defiance and self-assertion. The novel's inversion of the conventional prairie-tale particularly bears on the fact that by becoming a breeder of pigs, Judith is trying to come to terms with the Oedipal relationship she had with her father. Depicted as an Old-Testamental patriarch, Judith's father is a symbol of authority and genealogy, who used to treat his daughter ("Daddy's girl") like the son he never had. Even as a teenager, Judith found it hard to get any satisfaction from her dates since she would always subconsciously look for her father in the boys she went out with and she would invariably find the boys inadequate. It is only after he has died and she has acquired her own farm that Judith realizes that "It was really [her father] she [had] wanted" all along (117). She more or less forces herself to go out with Jim, the neighbors' son, but their relationship is seriously hampered by the fact that through her unconventional, provocative behavior she constantly flies in the face of the local rednecks.

Judith's quest for self-fulfilment culminates in the scene where he castrates the young boars. Though more than a little daunted by the hog-breeding Circe, Jim has offered to castrate the piglets for her since he believes that it is clearly not something a woman can or should do. However, with Judith looking on while he is carrying out "the castration of his own sex" (167), Jim loses heart and messes up, and Judith is forced to take over:

> She reached out her hand, now sure and fearless, so perfectly knowing. "Give me that [scalpel] and you hold this pig down." She shifted and the piglet felt her weight transfer, felt heavier bones settle over him. And then she was wiping his scrotum with a warm, strong-smelling wet cloth, and then there was the slice, quick and clean, the piglet's furious shriek on the heels of it, Judith slicing at the membranes of his testicles while he fought away from her knife, wriggling and squealing. And she slipped them out of him so easily, so swiftly presiding over his emasculation like the savage witch of pragmatism that she was. . . .
> She castrated them all. Swift and cruel she pierced them, slicing so fast there was hardly time for blood to flow, flicking their testicles onto the floor of the chorehouse like offending parasites. (166)

This episode finally liberates Judith from the anger and frustration that have crippled her life and her relations with men till now: "she was free" (170). Shortly after, in a passage revealing the novel's indebtedness, both in theme and language, to D.H. Lawrence's *The Rainbow*, Judith takes the initiative to consummate her relationship with Jim, a gesture that is meant to symbolize her triumph over herself, or rather, over the self that men—notably her father—had created for her:

> And oh yes, it was very good. There was something about denying her childishness that made it better than it had ever been, the length of him inside her shucking away all those years like so much chaff, and she was pounding his back with her fists and in the barn the pigs heard it and knew, her drawnout wail filtering through the wood like the announcement of a terrible birth, and she lay quiet at last under the thud thud thud of his still and beating body, her hands beside her open and relaxed. (175)

However, like the boar she hires for her sow Marie Antoinette, men have only a "limited usefulness" (177) for Judith. Still, there is every suggestion that she has at last found her place and her life: breeding pigs, with a man at her beck and call in the neighboring farm for those moments whenever she needs to be confirmed in what D.H. Lawrence would call her "essential womanhood."

Van Herk's inversion of the western myth (the earth-father being replaced by an earth-mother) is thus in the final analysis not really an inversion at all. While her castrating the pigs is clearly meant to celebrate Judith's triumph over the male sex (woman over her lover, daughter over father, earth-mother over earth-father), she can still only define herself and her womanhood as inverted manhood. She has managed to discard her old identity of "Daddy's girl," only to find herself being redefined as a cowgirl (or rather, a female pigbreeder). Thus Judith remains caught up in a gender economy that is dominated by men and maleness: mere inversion reconfirms rather than reconstructs gender-related value systems. Judith's quest for her essential selfhood does not take her west of conventional womanhood: it just pins her down even more firmly on an isolated farm, somewhere just outside of Norberg, breeding pigs.

While in *Judith* Van Herk offers us a revisionist, geofeminist retelling of the classical myth of Circe—a sort of porcine version of "even cowgirls get the blues"—in her second novel, *The Tent Peg* (1981) she refurbishes the Biblical story of the prophetess Deborah, as told in chapters 4 and 5 of the Book of Judges.[2] Thus the novel's heroine is a young woman who renamed herself "J.L." because people used to always mispronounce the name her religious parents had given her, "Jael," after the Heber's wife. The overriding image in the novel's symbolism, the tent peg, is a reference to the nail with which Jael kills Sisera, captain of the host of Jabin, the king of Canaan, thereby freeing the children of Israel from its oppressor. J.L.'s identification with her Old-Testamental namesake becomes most apparent when J.L.'s friend, the singer Deborah, sends her a victory song that is almost literally taken from the Bible (223). The parallels with Old Testamental myth may be clear and consistent, but in the final analysis they constitute a rather cumbersomely ostentatious presence in what is, after all, a realistic novel about a young woman fighting a very modern battle against the prejudices of male chauvinism.

Determined to "head for nowhere and to look at everything in [her] narrow world from a detached distance" for a while (23), J.L. joins a team of geologists who are about to set out on a prospecting trip into the Yukon mountains. However, prospecting in the wild wastes of the Canadian Northwest being an exclusively and intensely male activity, the price she has to pay in order to get hired—as the crew's bush cook—is high: she has to disguise herself as a man and therefore to suppress her female identity. Fortunately, the crew's leader, Mackenzie, is open-minded enough not to fire her after he has discovered that she is in fact a woman.

Thus nine men and one woman are flown to the Wernecke mountains, where they pitch their summer camp. Soon tensions begin to rise as J.L., by her mere presence more than by her actual behaviour, begins to upset the traditional male economy within the prospectors' team. Her main adversary is a blunt vindictive man named Jerome who believes that geology is "a man's field" and that women in a camp are "bad for morale" (27, 28). The others initially keep their distance, mystified as they are by the fact that J.L. conspicuously eludes conventional notions of femininity: not only does she have a man's name and a manly physique, but she turns out to be a great shot, drink beer and spirits from the bottle, crack jokes, beat the men at poker, and have no fear at all of flying in the helicopter. Soon, however, the men begin to appreciate the female touch that J.L. has added to life in the camp, and they begin to move closer and closer to her. From kitchen witch she gradually turns into an earth-mother, protecting the men from themselves and each other, hearing their confessions, healing their wounded souls, and enlightening them generally in gender-political terms. In the words of one of the men: "She's like a pillar in the middle of the camp. We all shuffle around her, matrixed" (168). More and more J.L. turns out to be a woman with a mission, revealing the feminist agenda that underlies Van Herk's novel: "I find myself waiting angrily," she says in an inner monologue addressed to her friend Deborah, "for that promised period of peace. I'm beginning to think that unless we take some action ourselves, it may never come. It's time we laid our hands on the workman's mallet and put the tent pegs to the sleeping temples, if ever we are going to get any rest" (173).

While the men are thus duly "fed and . . . confessed and . . . redeemed" by J.L. (214), it is only Jerome that persists in his aggressive rejection of her. After his attempt to oust Mackenzie, and with him J.L., from the camp has turned into a humiliating fiasco, Jerome decides the time has come to put the "little bitch" in her place and take her down "a peg or two" (218). Forcing his way into her tent one night, he tries to rape her, threatening her with his Magnum. She quite easily manages to disarm him, however, and turns the table on him. Pointing the gun at his crotch, she threatens to castrate him and to, in turn, take *him* down a peg or two. As it happens, she is magnanimous enough to spare the "six inches of ludicrous, dangling flesh [that gives him] strength, power" (137); besides, castrating Jerome probably would not change his attitude toward women anyway.

J.L.'s moral victory over Jerome and male chauvinism in general is appropriately marked by the victory song which she receives from Deborah immediately after the dramatic event in her tent—the song in which she is put on a par with Jael, her Old-Testamental sister. The novel ends with J.L. dancing a rousing, celebratory victory dance on a table-top with the men all gathered around her in awe and fascination: "For a moment I can pretend I am Deborah celebrating myself, victory, peace regained. And in their faces I see my transfiguration, themselves transformed, each one with the tent peg through the temple cherishing the knowledge garnered in sleep, in unwitting trust" (226). Of all the men in the camp, however, it is Mackenzie who is singled out to receive J.L.'s special favors, and it is he who in the end turns out to have benefited the most from her healing powers:

> Ah Sisera, I would trade with you. I would give all I had to die at her hand, to have her offer me bread and milk, to feel her smoothing a rug over my tired frame and, yes, to lie asleep and innocent as she lays one hand on the mallet and the other on the tent peg and gently, oh so gently that I might never awake, nails me to the earth, pierces my ear, my temple, with her loving wrath and bestows on me respite, peace. (227)

According to Hartmut Lutz, within the context of the novel's gender conflict, the "peg" operates as "a symbol of female solidarity and female wisdom, to be conveyed to unenlightened males" (Meat 47); this reading, however, fails to take account of the fact that the so-called female wisdom that J.L. is supposed to possess is of a fairly crude nature, and that Jerome, as the unenlightened male that is to benefit most from this wisdom, is a caricature of maleness—unenlightened or otherwise—and hence resembles a straw man merely set up to be knocked over at the appropriate time.

As a matter of fact, even Lutz has to admit that the characters in Van Herk's novel ("except perhaps two") are all distinctly flat characters (Meat 46), and resemble in no way their more illustrious mythical counterparts in the Book of Judges. Not only is Jerome too blunt to be true, but Franklin, the poet, is a whining wimp; Milton, the churchy Mennonite, is made out to be naive and dim-witted beyond belief; Hearn, the photographer, literally has pictures on his brain every time he makes an appearance; and Mackenzie, we are led to believe, is still, after ten years, obsessively trying to figure out why his wife left him. In short, the characters are mere puppets dancing on the author's string; it is not very surprising, given the novel's geopolitical agenda, that the notions the men have about women are as predictable as their personalities. Thus Milton opines at one point, "I never seen a girl like her before. She is hard and angry-like instead of soft and still and holding inside the way a girl should be" (82); while Mackenzie muses, "It's inconceivable to me that I could have mistaken [J.L.] for a boy, she is every inch of her female, marvelously light and easy and quick, carrying the mystery that is only there in women. Because women are so mysterious, so blind and inward and silent, so tuned to vibrations that we have never been able to hear. They turn in faultless circles, they move like vases forming, always changing but always perfect" (145). However, J.L.'s notions about men turn out to be not very much more enlightened: in her eyes men always "blame a woman for everything, even his hormones," causing women to feel constantly "vulnerable, open to attack" and hence to be always on the defensive: "That's what we are, after all, we women. Survivors" (105; 190; 136).

Of course, we should be careful not to mix up a character's opinions with the author's, but that is not the point here: the point is that Van Herk employs her characters in an imaginative metaphorical framework that is supposed to represent and subsequently subvert a particular ideology of gender that privileges the male over the female, the cerebral over the visceral, and that within this framework over-simplifying and stereotyping a character's psychology and gendered behaviour beyond recognition and plausibility, seriously compromises, if not disqualifies, the ideological agenda that informs her writing. Equally, Van Herk's creation of J.L., the liberator of men, is (like Judith before her) too much inspired by a mere inversion of conventional female gender-tags to convincingly bring across the author's geofeminist politics. Van Herk's literary mentor Rudy Wiebe apparently once observed in a response to one of the novel's critics that *The Tent Peg* was conceived as a trap set for "obtuse males" (qtd. in Meat 65): presumably, it is a sign of the male reader's obtuseness if he takes umbrage at the outspokenness of the character of J.L. Given the lack of subtlety in Van Herk's representation of gender and gender-relations in *The Tent Peg*, it is not very surprising that the novel *would* trap obtuse (male) readers; more perceptive readers might want to regard the novel, in the words of

Lutz, as a "utopian, feminist dream"—neither politically relevant nor quite mythical.

Although in many ways yet another inversion of the myth of the west, Van Herk's third novel, *No Fixed Address* (1987), presents a rather more complex treatment of the concept of geofeminism. Taking its cue from such modern American myths as Kerouac's *On the Road* and Miller's play *Death of a Salesman*, *No Fixed Address* tells the story of Arachne Manteia, a traveling sales representative for "Ladies' Comfort Limited," a Winnipeg-based firm specializing in exclusive ladies' underwear. Driving a 1959 black Mercedes 300, Arachne travels across the Canadian west peddling her wares to unsuspecting store owners, whom she frequently shocks into buying her panties patterned with spiders or eggplants or pigs or skulls or texts like, "*A woman without a man is like a fish without a bicycle.*" Arachne has thus appropriated at least two of the traditional domains of the male hegemony: driving and selling lingerie.

Arachne performs both activities, however, with a vengeance. For where it is conventionally traveling salesmen who pick up women only to abandon them at some roadside motel, in *No Fixed Address* it is Arachne who uses men in much the same way. Describing herself as "amoral, selfish, [and] dishonest" (103), Arachne eats men raw, appreciating them only for the physical performance in bed (or, more typically, on the back seat of her Mercedes): "They're just bodies, you could put a paper bag over their heads," she tells her friend Thena (33). And although she is the company's top underwear "salesman," she does not, as a matter of principle, wear any herself, because, as the (female) omniscient narrator explains to us in the prologue,

> *For centuries women have suffered the discomfort of corsets, padding, petticoats, girdles, bustles, garters and bust pads. The trimmings too contributed: buckles that chafed the tender skin of the ribcage, hooks and eyes of dubious connection, front-closing snaps on uplift bras that released at inappropriate moments; the sucking rasp of elastic, spandex that relaxed too soon, itchy lace. . . . It is a wonder that we can still walk. And who will be responsible for what those tortures have created? The existence of smelling salts, hysteria, frigidity and shrewishness can all be attributed to uncomfortable underwear.* (9-10; italics in original)

It comes as no surprise that Arachne, the Spider Woman, who as a fifteen-year-old was the leader and sole female member of a street gang called the Black Widows, peddles these symbols of female suppression merely to lure lustful men into her web, where, once caught, she will suck them empty and cast their spent bodies aside.

Although she has a steady relationship with Thomas, a cartographer with a nine-to-five job who tries to turn her into "a respectable woman" (137), Arachne is seldom at home with him in their house in Calgary. Rather, she makes use of the maps that he draws of the prairies and the Rocky Mountains to set off again for the unexplored landscapes of the Canadian west:

> From Calgary roads spider over the prairie. Arachne pores over Thomas' maps, the lines enticing her to quest beyond the city's radius. She gets into the car and sets the bonnet toward the sun. She is learning travel, the pace and progression of journey, the multifarious seduction of movement.... Arachne travels to travel (163-64).

After many adventures involving an endless string of "road jockeys," a robbery, a kidnapping, and a rape-attempt, Arachne finds herself in Vancouver again, the city where she used to live and work as a bus driver before she met Thomas. Ostensibly running from the police but really running from Thomas and her own history, she is determined to cross to Vancouver Island, "go as far west as the road and the ocean allow, farther than anyone will think of following" (281). Before she gets on the ferry, however, she visits a Sushi restaurant, where the chef prepares her some "fugu," a kind of fish whose guts contain a deadly nerve poison. While the fugu-ritual does not actually kill her, Arachne—following in this her namesake in Ovid's *Metamorphoses*—does experience a change of identity: "I died, she thinks. I'm dead. I was eating fugu. I can kill you" (285). Indeed, kill is what she does, for as a man on the ferry to Vancouver Island starts to fondle her breasts, she sticks a hatpin all the way into his heart, after which she walks straight back to "the black hump of her Mercedes," her spider's shell (287).[3]

Having finally reached the point furthest west on Vancouver Island, Arachne still is not free; she has come to "the edge of the world" (293), but she does not fall off. So she drives back to the mainland and then turns north, and keeps on driving, till she is picked up by two geologists who kidnap her in a helicopter and take her even farther north. In a postscript to the novel, an unnamed narrator (Thomas?) tries to retrace her steps, but after a fruitless search finds himself ultimately heading for the Mackenzie Mountains that separate the Yukon and the Northwest Territories: *"You have fallen off the edge. There is no ocean or continent beyond, only the enormity of spectrum and range and latitude, of, dear God, four-dimensional nothingness"* (317; italics in original). The only trace that Arachne has left is a trail of Ladies' Comfort panties along the road north: *"There is no end to the panties; there will be no end to this road"* (319; italics in original).

The implication is that Arachne has finally managed to shed all that used to tie her down to an identity, a job, a relationship, a sex; that, in short, she has gone "west of Woman". In this sense Arachne's life story is an advancement on Judith's, which never progressed beyond a simple reversal of gender roles. Yet does Arachne's escape into "four-dimensional nothingness"—death, presumably—really constitute a solution to the problem of female self-realization in a male dominated discursive environment? According to Van Herk her heroine's exploration of death is "not deathly." Death, Van Herk claims, is "only another country" and Arachne is not so much "struggling to get herself . . . killed [as] 'died'" (Jones 11, 10). The trope of a woman realizing her full potential by crossing the boundary of "the forbidden male territory of death" may have proved its rhetorical usefulness in some contemporary feminist writing, but it lacks persuasive force here (Jones 11).[4] Arachne may at the end of the novel be striking out for geographically new territory, but what does this really mean when we never hear from her again? Far from subversively turning absence into a presence, Van Herk seems to relegate her heroine to a realm of non-being, thereby leaving the existing ideological hegemony untouched. For a writer who takes pride in labeling herself a "political feminist," this position comes awkwardly close to an elitist play of words. Hence I do not share Goldman's comment that *No Fixed Address* constitutes "Van Herk's feminist, militaristic strategy for infiltrating and destabilizing the masculine terrain" (26). By having her heroine disappear into "four-dimensional nothingness," Van Herk places her heroine (and herself) outside any engagement whatsoever with the masculine terrain. Significantly, at the end of the day, Arachne finds herself, in the words of the author, "selling underwear in the realms of the dead, where people certainly don't need it" (Jones 12).

In *Judith* and *No Fixed Address* Van Herk may rail against men for having forced women, over the centuries, to pluck their eyebrows and to lace up their bodies in various items of uncomfortable clothing; in *Places Far From Ellesmere* she claims that men have not only always tried to control women, but that they have actually *invented* them. Taking her cue from Tolstoy's creation of the character of Anna Karenina, undoubtedly one of the nineteenth century's most notorious cases of constructed womanhood, Van Herk sets out to explore the issue of male appropriation and distortion (even violation) of female identity. She charges Tolstoy with having "writ[ten] Anna no choices" (8), as a result of which she has become "a self-indulgent character created by a man who couldn't imagine women enacting anything more interesting than adultery or motherhood. Prescripted choices: mothers, saints or whores" (81).

The quintessential victim of male imperialism, Anna Karenina becomes the reference point for the author's *un*reading and *re*writing of her past, her personal geography, her childhood, youth and adulthood, in three places "far from Ellesmere": Edberg, the village where she was born and grew up in; Edmonton, where she attended the University of Alberta; and Calgary, where she lived for a while after graduating from university. Exploring the cross-pollination between space and language, the novel thus becomes a "fiction of geography/geography of fiction: [the] coming together in people and landscape and the harboured designations of fickle memory. Invented: textual: un/read: the hieroglyphic secrets of the past" (40). Inevitably, however, in the wake of the mapping of spaces and the naming of identity come the invading of the land and the invading of the self. Hence the author's desperate desire to flee Calgary, "this growing graveyard" (74), and to seek asylum in the desolate and uncharted terrain of Ellesmere Island.

It is here, in the unmapped, perpetually frozen whiteness of this Arctic desert, that the author hopes to re/discover her unwritten, unlanguaged self, as well as to set Anna Karenina free from Tolstoy's prison-house of language. "Ellesmere," the author emphasizes, is "the consummate escape," both for Anna and for herself, because it is "absence," a "tabula rasa," where the coordinates of time and space are in abeyance, and where hence language, that distorting presence, is turned adrift (77). The only mapped identity that she "permits" herself to take with her is Tolstoy's *Anna Karenina* (79), "this corpulent Russian novel that pretended for so long to read the essential psyche of the passionate woman succumbing to extreme and impossible passions, infecting all around her" (91). According to Van Herk, Tolstoy is a writer who beats

> his character into submission, the very text alien to her, her story. The fiction impossible to read, stuffed into a gunnysack, rummaged, constantly searched, fumbled, a kind of physical ransacking. In the same way is Anna rummaged, fumbled, groped by Tolstoy, her passions and inclinations jumbled together in his gunnysack, roughly thrown over the shoulder and carted on an extended pilgrimage to represent the fate of wayward women. (117-18)

Reducing Tolstoy's artistic status from that of an authority on the deeper stirrings of the female soul to a dirty old man "rummag[ing] in Anna's bedroom, in the secret precincts of her passionate world" (117), the author is determined to "un/read her, [to] set her free" from her "paginated presence . . . and offer her alternatives" (82; 77):

> You must free her from the constraints of the novel she has been imprisoned in, shake her loose from the pages of her own story so that she can float over the landscape here in this landscape of a woman, this northern body, waiting to fall in love. You are in love with Ellesmere. (131-32).

In "reading" *Anna Karenina* "beyond language," the author, presumably, vicariously liberates herself from the shackles of masculinist discourse.

In her essay "In Visible Ink" Van Herk works out the trope of identity as an "absent presence" in more explicit detail and in a way that helps elucidate the concept as used in her novel and in her geofeminist project in general. In the essay Van Herk states at one point that

> Even more extreme is the illusion of absence that is truly presence, tremendous presence, with no need to articulate itself narcissistically, being so much a *hereness*. This space, this landscape, this temperature, question all *document* and instead document me, without reference to an other; decipherable as glass I am, and fragile as any silenced voice, a tracement of arctic essence. No comparisons possible, no contrast available for measurement or ruler for diversity. This north is the gauge, and all else divergence. I am effaced,

become an enunciative field, a page untouched by pen, no archive and no history. Happily. (*In Visible* 8)

The climax of her Arctic experience as described in this essay comes when her Inuik guide, Pijamini, describes the landscape of Ellesmere to the author in Inuktitut, a language which she does not understand—thus taking her beyond language and beyond herself: "He gives me *his* words, and thus names me, writes my invisible and unlanguaged self into his archaeology. I am written, finally, with that nomadic language" (10). This passage signals a major hitch in Van Herk's politics of language; it is ironic that the person who frees her from words and thus liberates her from her old, languaged self is both a man and her "leader" (9), and that this patriarchal figure of power represents her in a language that might well be as hostile to her female identity as the language she is familiar with.

This problematizes Van Herk's feminist agenda when she subsequently extends her experience of discovering her self within a geography and a language she does not know into a statement about reading and writing in general:

> Reader, this amulet of the first and most final of all crypto-frictions [that is, her essay "In Visible Ink"] is that one can be disappeared and re-written in a language beyond one's own. Herein resides the ultimate illusion of text: you are not reading me but writing, not me but yourself; you are not reading writing but being read, a live text in a languaging world. (10)

Leaving aside the fact that these remarks sound like faint echoes of observations made by at least half a dozen poststructuralist language theorists in the seventies and eighties (Barthes, Derrida, Foucault), a statement like, "one can be disappeared and re-written in a language beyond one's own," simply does not carry any power of conviction. Why would one want to be re-written in a language which one does not understand? What would it be to the "other" re-writing you in his or her language? And what would it be to oneself? And how can one be re-written in "a language beyond one's own" when, as she indicates in the passage just quoted, all language is a mirror of the self? Indeed, can there *be* "a language beyond one's own"? It would take us beyond the confines of this essay and into the abstract realm of High Deconstruction to settle these language issues in any kind of detail, but even without doing so, it is clear that in passages like the above Van Herk is dangerously close to solipsistic word-play and to narcissistically indulging in the echoes of her own musings. It will be more fruitful to address Van Herk's position toward what is often referred to in feminist studies as the "politics of location."

According to the biographical notice in *No Fixed Address*, Van Herk is interested "in the unexplored landscapes of Canada, as well as the unexplored areas of human myth and possibility. A regionalist and a feminist, she works through her fiction to rediscover lost stories and myths within contemporary time and space" (320); judging from her latest novel, however, she may be interested in visiting these unexplored landscapes and myths, but she does not appear to want to share with the reader what she finds there: "Ellesmere," Van Herk writes in a dedication prefacing the novel, "will stay, eternally, mysteriously, its own geografictione" (5). What, one wonders, does this "Ellesmere" mean in practical (geo)feminist political terms, if we do not know what or where it is?

Ultimately, Van Herk's exploration of the uncharted, nomadic terrain west of conventional representations of Woman falls short of its objectives on account of a fundamental ambivalence in her geofeminist project. Ideologically, she remains stranded between two incompatible positions: on the one hand the (for many feminists) politically untenable position characterized by—to adapt one of Melville's phrases—"Silence is the only Voice of Woman," and on the other the equally problematic simple inversion of gender roles. Van Herk wavers between wanting to escape beyond language and trying to colonize the male terrain by appropriating male discourse and destabilizing its representations of woman: while the former position will effectively deliver Van Herk into the hands of male imperialism bound and gagged, the latter will inevitably mean that she will have to compromise and thus run the risk of being assimilated into the very ideology she is trying to subvert.

Perhaps we should not, as Marlene Goldman suggests at the end of her analysis of *No Fixed Address*, come down too hard on Van Herk for falling short of her geofeminist objectives (36); after all, what she is up against in her writings is a well-known and unresolvable poststructuralist dilemma: if she were to succeed in describing the "unexplored beyond" (of language and of her self), it would no longer be an "unexplored beyond," which would mean that in order to preserve her female identity she would have to strike out for a further beyond, and so on—*a mise-en-abyme* if ever there was one. This would leave Van Herk's writing continually on the verge of disappearing into "four-dimensional nothingness."

This in itself would not perhaps be such a bad position for an artist to be in — one is reminded, for instance, of Nietzsche's observation, "No artist tolerates reality," and of William Blake's motto, "I must invent my own system or else be enslaved by other men's." Van Herk's attempts to construct an uncharted space of resistance, where questions of identity and power can be addressed in new and liberatory ways, make considerable sense from a theoretical point of view. Indeed, Van Herk's geofeminism takes up a concern that is central to much of contemporary feminist theory: thus, it taps directly into Teresa de Lauretis's mapping of a strategic "elsewhere" — "the elsewhere of discourse here and now, the blind spots, or the space-off, of its representations" (*Technologies* 25) and into Gillian Rose's more recent work on the concept of "paradoxical space" — which she defines as "a space imagined in order to articulate a troubled relation to the hegemonic discourses of masculinism" (159). However, if Van Herk's writing was inspired by these or similar concepts of gendered space, then her geofeminist agenda is problematic for at least two reasons.

First, in the novels discussed above, Van Herk is first and foremost "an award-winning Canadian novelist," not a writer of feminist theory, and the two, I suggest, do not mix very well, at least not in a single discourse. De Lauretis's concept of "space-off" may work very well as a strategic tool within feminist ideological discourse, but in trying to *narrativize* such a theoretical concept, Van Herk is in effect attempting to fuse the imaginary and the metaphorical with the analytical and the argumentative, thereby ultimately achieving neither — which, I believe, becomes particularly apparent in *Places Far From Ellesmere* and, to a lesser degree, in *No Fixed Address*. Of course, I am not saying here that narrative discourse and feminist ideology do not go together: all I am saying is that writing a feminist *critique* is not the same as writing a feminist *novel*; not surprisingly, perhaps, Van Herk's geofeminism is brought out much more convincingly in *In Visible Ink* than in *Places Far From Ellesmere*. According to Van Herk the antagonistic critical response that her work sometimes elicited in the past was the result of critics resenting her replacing the traditional "Woman" of masculinist discourse by what she called a "strong, devil-may-care woman" (Jones 12-13); however, she should seriously consider the possibility that these critics may not have been so much shocked as unimpressed by her heroines. If Van Herk wants to be a "fictioneer" who "transform[s] particular worlds into fiction" (Jones 7; 10), she should do just that and not get entangled in fictionalized theoretical discourse.

Second, De Lauretis's positioning of her "elsewhere" beyond the limits of masculinist discourse differs in a crucial respect from Van Herk's in the sense that where De Lauretis emphatically defines her "elsewhere of discourse" as "spaces in the margins of hegemonic discourses, social spaces carved in the interstices of institutions and in the chinks and cracks of the power-knowledge apparati" (*Technologies* 25), Van Herk, notably in her two latest novels and in some of the essays in *In Visible Ink*, writes herself completely *off* the map of the hegemonic masculinist discourse of identity (in her efforts to escape from its prescriptive pressure). Given that in the novel she effectively rules out the possibility of a return to the old, pre-Ellesmere world, Van Herk's eulogy of Anna Karenina acquires distinctly fatalistic and even morbid overtones as her narrator's identification with the victim of Tolstoy's misogynist pryings and proddings becomes complete and her paranoia of the masculine is sublimated into an overwhelming death wish:

> At last, again, you think you've found a home.
> You search out possible sites for your future grave....
> You are destined to become ashes. Ashes alone. There are murderers at large....
> Your wanderings have passed. explorations on site, a site through which to read, to welcome death, early or late. (140-41)

The atmosphere of necromantic narcissism that hangs over the final scenes in the novel merely goes to show how easily the rendering of the concept of an "absent presence" or an "elsewhere of discourse" in imaginative, metaphorical terms may go off the rails. Van Herk's claim that her fiction "offers a trajectory into the forbidden, into magic, into death, into sexuality, the very elements of life we are most curious about and most afraid of" hardly justifies her giving up telling a convincing tale altogether, as she does in *Places Far From Ellesmere* (Jones 9). "Fiction ought to be suggestive," Van Herk once remarked; "It ought to suggest to us alternatives" (Jones 13): indeed, but suggesting or imag(in)ing an alternative is not the same as *stating* it. Literature that does that is destined to become ashes —

something, paradoxically, Van Herk knows full well: "Emotion . . . without human recognition . . . is meaningless. Language gives meaning to passion" (*Frozen* 84).

Acknowledgment

I would like to thank Amanda Gilroy, who saw this essay through its final versions and provided valuable suggestions for revision.

Notes

1. I use the term "Woman" here, as well as in the title of this essay, as defined by Teresa de Lauretis, signifying the masculinist fantasy figure of the "imagined feminine." See her *Technologies of Gender*, notably 1-30.
2. For an extensive discussion of the mythological references in *The Tent Peg*, see Lutz 1989.
3. A more detailed reading of this scene can be found in, H. Lutz and J. Hindersmann 1991: 19-20.
4. For an exhaustive discussion of the relation between femininity and death, see Elisabeth Bronfen's *Over Her Dead Body: Death, Femininity and the Aesthetic*.

JEANETTE LYNES   *Lakehead University*

Is Newfoundland Inside that T.V.?

Regionalism, Postmodernism, and Wayne Johnston's Human Amusements

How compatibly do the regional and the postmodern co-exist in Canadian novels? In many cases, strongly region-identified novelists seem to have found literary postmodernism's various modes of disruption or discontinuity and its predilection towards metafiction less than appealing. The reasons for this are probably complex, and numerous factors surrounding literary production in this country undoubtedly come into play. For instance, most authors who live and work "out in the regions" — that is, far from Toronto or Montreal — typically gain initial exposure to their work in a localized context likely to be less diverse than these metropolitan centres in terms of audience composition and taste. Sharing this context are regional presses, no doubt equally sensitive to their cultural milieu. Other factors include how individual novelists position themselves in relation to their respective locales, and the extent to which the issue of place plays a role in their work at all.

Nevertheless, it is possible to identify novels which bring together aspects of both the regional and the postmodern. Sheila Watson's *The Double Hook*, Robert Kroetsch's *Badlands* and *The Studhorse Man*, and George Bowering's *Burning Water* demonstrate felicitous unions of these "isms." But a much longer list of regional novels that are not postmodern can be readily compiled, especially when one considers writing from Atlantic Canada. "Postmodern" is hardly a term one feels compelled to ascribe to work by David Adams Richards, Alistair MacLeod, Percy Janes or Sheldon Currie. Ray Smith's *Cape Breton is the Thought Control Centre of*

Canada is certainly regional and postmodern, but hardly classifiable as a novel.

It would be as misleading to infer from this that Atlantic novelists have somehow disavowed postmodernism, for such an inference would assume that these authors invariably write about "the maritime experience"—in other words, that their work is consistently informed by a kind of regional determinism. The work of Newfoundland author Wayne Johnston, whose writing bears the stamp of both regionalism and postmodernism, exemplifies a unique intermingling of these two sensibilities: especially, their impact on each other. His 1994 novel *Human Amusements* embraces strategies often identified with postmodernism, strategies such as parody and a sense of playful intertextuality. At the same time, Johnston's narrative registers genuine, even apocalyptic, alarm in relation to a central feature of postmodern culture, electronic media, and the damaging effects it can have on our sense of origins, identity and place. Thus, his "T.V. novel" forms a compelling site for examining the intersection of regionalism, postmodernism and globalism, given the corporatizing, globalizing agendas of electronic communications in a postmodern era.

As critics like Lynne Joyrich, taking her cue from Baudrillard and Jameson, see it, television occupies a key position within postmodern culture (29). Johnston's novel, too, recognizes T.V.'s supremacy as a mode of entertainment or "amusement," but his narrative also alerts us to the perils of postmodernist mass culture, specifically, its tendency to eradicate differences of various kinds. Perhaps Johnston does not go as far as Neil Postman, who claims that we are "amusing ourselves to death," but Johnston nevertheless demonstrates how media can constitute, to quote Postman, a kind of "prison culture" and "thought-control" (155).

The fact that, as Joshua Meyrowitz has compellingly argued, electronic media have reshaped, and continue to reshape, our sense of place in radical ways, emphasizes the importance of examining the new (postmodern) technology in relation to regionalist concerns. Johnston examines this relationship in fictional form, and in *Human Amusements* melds together a skeptical postmodernism with a subliminal regionalism.

Meyrowitz contends that media technology—and he includes under this rubric devices such as television, videos, computers, telephones,—undermines traditional spatial boundaries, a result which, in turn, alters social relationships in significant ways. "We lose our old 'sense of place'" (ix), he writes, commenting as well that the physical structures that once divided our society into many distinct spatial settings for interaction have been greatly reduced in social significance. The walls of the family home, for example, are no longer effective barriers that wholly isolate the family from the larger community and society. (i)

Later he adds, "In many ways, electronic media have homogenized places and experiences and have become common denominators that link all of us" (viii). Since regionalism is surely part of the discourse of place, it seems likely that the "homogenization" of place Meyrowitz identifies could include the disappearance of distinct locale. Postmodern theorists like Frederich Jameson have similarly identified a collapse of spatial boundaries and concepts such as inside and outside, as part of, to recall Lyotard's phrase, "the postmodern condition." The question Johnston's novel invites us to consider, then, is whether it is even possible to sustain a sense of place, a "regional" identity, within a world of collapsing spatial boundaries and postmodern, electronic media. This concern over the status of the regional within a global, technological context situates Johnston's novel within one of the central debates of the late twentieth century.

Johnston's novel is essentially about the longing for a lost place—an elegiac story about the demise of region. And despite the novel's universalizing title, the problems presented in the narrative can be seen as distinctly regional in nature. In a gesture of craftiness, however, Johnston removes—or, at first glance, seems to remove—the regional from the equation altogether, in *Human Amusements*, by setting the novel in Toronto, the city in which he himself now resides. Johnston's endeavor to distance himself from the regional is also apparent in his 1994 interview with Bruce Porter. Johnston states here, "I don't think of literature in regional terms no matter how big the region is.... Nor is it necessary to put those kinds of labels on writers at all" (Porter 27; 16). Ironically, these remarks appear in Newfoundland's *Tickle Ace*, one of Canada's most ardently regional journals.

It is perhaps not surprising that Johnston's attitude towards regionalism exhibits ambivalence, given the habitual marginalization of Newfoundland literature in critical accounts of Canadian writing. Johnston's wariness of being classified as a regional writer continues in the same interview. For example, despite the grounding of his best-known novel, *The Story of*

Bobby O'Malley, in a specific milieu, Johnston says, "I don't think it's a regional book" (Porter 17). Nevertheless, *Bobby O'Malley* achieves many of its comic effects by virtue of its author's close knowledge of a particular place, and by his skill in pitting the eccentricity of a Newfoundland family—the O'Malleys—against certain norms or standards in the domestic, religious, and social fabric of the island's culture.

Thus while Johnston endeavors to distance himself from the potentially restrictive or even dismissive connotations that the "regional" designation has for him, and indeed has had for other authors, he nevertheless recognizes the influence of place on his work, remarking that even though he has never set out to "write regionally," "that doesn't mean Newfoundland isn't there in other ways, ways that are common to living on an island, in an isolated place away from the centre" (Porter 17). The phrase "there in other ways" provides a clue for discerning Johnston's subliminal regionalism in *Amusements*, the story of his postmodern family, the television Prendergasts, which unfolds in the central Canadian urban world of the 1960s and '70s.

My contention that Johnston, in *Amusements*, continues to explore regional issues in a subliminal manner is supported, as well, by his assertion that he sees his 'T.V. novel' as "a kind of complementary book to *The Story of Bobby O'Malley*," which "plays out completely some of the things just touched on in *Bobby O'Malley*" (Porter 19). The focus in *Amusements* remains that of a single-child family marked as "different" from those around them. The Prendergasts, like the O'Malleys, Johnston states, "are an isolated family" (Porter 19). What *Amusements*, using the family to represent localized identity, "plays out completely" is Johnston's fascination with islands—in this case, metaphorical ones—and with the power differential of regional difference and smallness pitted against the powerful, homogenizing forces of corporate culture.

The idea of smallness reminds us that both *The Story of Bobby O'Malley* and *Human Amusements* are, after all, novels about childhood. And herein lies another element which supports a reading of *Amusements* as an exploration of regionalism-in-crisis. In his essay, "Images of Prairie Man," Eli Mandel contends that regional literature may be a literature of childhood, stating that the child's vision

> is of home; and that surely is the essence of what we mean by a region, the overpowering feeling of nostalgia associated with the

> place we know as the first place, the first vision of things, the first clarity of things. . . . The child, then, is the focus of nostalgia for the place that was—and regional literature is then a literature of the past. (206)

Johnston's novelistic style consists of an eclectic blending of comedy, satire, parody, pathos and, not least of all, a sense of sadness and nostalgia. The longing for a lost familial harmony, a missing father, and a simpler life haunts Johnston's boy protagonist Henry Prendergast in *Amusements*, as he is catapulted into an increasingly fragmented and complex technological way of life: in short, as Henry becomes a famous television star, he moves further and further away from the "first place," from his family's modest home on St. Clair Avenue and its distinct region of childhood safety and quaintly primitive technology (as opposed to the comparatively sophisticated technology he later encounters). Looking back on his earlier life, Henry, the novel's first-person narrator, remarks, "For me the early days of television are the early days of everything" (3) and, with a distinct tone of nostalgia, "This [the St. Clair home] was the life that, soon, we would leave behind" (9).

What destroys the "first place," the more pure world of childhood—and, in Mandel's terms, regionality—is clearly related to media technology in Johnston's narrative. Indeed, as Meyrowitz argues, in addition to spatial boundaries, media has dissolved traditional familial roles, including the very distinction between child and adult. In the newly configured familial roles brought on largely by media, "father" becomes anachronistic:

> the analysis presented here suggests that both the rise and fall of childhood and the decline and rise of women's rights and involvement in the public sphere may be closely linked to major shifts in communication technology in the past and in our own time. The spread of literacy, with its emphasis on hierarchy and sequence, supported a linear chain of command, from God-the-father, through a strong central national leader, to a father who was a god to his wife and children. As new means of communication blur hierarchy and sequence in our own time, we are experiencing a reintegration of many splintered roles. (314)

Meyrowitz's comments resonate closely with Johnston's T.V. family, in that traditional gender roles are radically shifted because of media technology; what Johnston's novel reveals is a nostalgia for the traditional "hierarchy," with the important "twist" of the father in *Amusements* being an artist—a struggling, angst-ridden writer. Ultimately, then, Johnston's novel not only explores the place of the regional in a globalizing postmodern world, but also the place of the artist/writer and print culture itself in an ever-expanding camera or screen culture—the world of television and video. Meyrowitz also suggests that the traditionally romantic notion of the artist may itself be endangered by media technology, remarking that new behaviour patterns caused by "new, synthesized behaviours" (310) mean the end of "many people's 'special' behaviours. . . . Gone are the great eccentrics, the passionate overpowering loves, the massive unrelenting hates" (311). The notion of the disappearance of the "great eccentrics" is especially germane to the father figures in Johnston's fiction: specifically Ted O'Malley and Peter Prendergast, artist figures who seem anachronistic and out of step with the worlds in which they live, even though, in the case of Ted O'Malley, they may appear to engage with media technology.

In *Human Amusements*, T.V. becomes an E.J. Pratt monster, the "Great Panjandrum" of the postmodern world, and his little family is, for a time, forced to dance to its rhythms. To briefly outline *Amusements*' plot, the Prendergast mother, Audrey, launches a successful television show called "Rumpus Room," in which she plays Miss Mary and her son Henry plays, alternatively, Bee Good and Bee Bad. After several years, she launches the even more successful "Philo Farnsworth Show," again starring her son Henry as Philo, the Idaho boy who invented the first electrical T.V. During the period in which this show becomes a smash hit, Peter, the Prendergast father—also a struggling novelist—becomes increasingly marginalized within the family, since fame and fortune belong exclusively to his wife and son. He remains staunchly detached from, and cynical about, his wife's and son's T.V. endeavors. Much of the narrative's energy is derived from this three-point tension, in which the mother embraces the culture of the screen image, Peter remains an advocate of "literature," or print culture, and Henry, the son, occupies an ambivalent position, mediating between the two poles his parents represent.

Given that television symbolizes the seductive but sinister sway held by centralizing, postmodern corporate culture, *Amusements* can be read as a cautionary tale of the damaging effects national and/or multi-national (in either case, read anti-regional) cultural production can have on a distinct locales (for example, islands and families). Johnston seems at once fascinated with the communications technology boom from the mid-twentieth century onward, yet aware of the ultimate morbidity of its power of image manipulation and its tendency to bankrupt artistic individualism.

This double-edged attitude of participation and critique is also revealed in terms of the way America functions in the narrative. On one level, the novel ostensibly participates in the heady excitement of U.S. expansionism; Johnston openly acknowledges that primary sources for his story include George Everson's *The Story of Television: The Life of Philo T. Farnsworth*, Joseph H. Udelson's *The Great Television Race: A History of the American Television Industry 1925-1941*, and Erik Barnouw's *Tube of Plenty: The Evolution of American Television*. However, Johnston does not simply retell an American story, but rather subverts the classic American rags-to-riches narrative. One way this subversion works is through a kind of incremental satire; as the protagonist Henry grows up and feels increasingly manipulated by his "T.V. mother" and program managers, the novel becomes darker and more apocalyptic in both subject matter and tone. Also, the Prendergasts' rags-to-riches story contains, as Johnston himself says, "about ten different kinds of parody" (Porter 19). One narrative being parodied is the Horatio Alger story. Johnston also plays with the Faustian story; his Mr. Mack represents a corporate world Mephistopheles who seduces Henry into an opportunity for mega-stardom. Orwell's *1984* is paradoxically echoed in Peter Prendergast's comment that "Big Mother is watching" (29) you, in reference to his wife's role as Miss Mary on her first T.V. show "Rumpus Room," which is itself a parodic version of Romper Room, a popular show for pre-schoolers during the novel's time period.

Parody, then—what Linda Hutcheon identifies as a distinctive trait of Canadian postmodern fiction (7)—facilitates Johnston's distancing from American industrial expansionism. Also, his exuberant immersion in the "research" of Americana is really a bit of a ruse, given that his novel culminates in a techno-apocalypse, an *attack* upon the capitalist myth of progress. Johnston ultimately looks at the North American society of image consumers from the edges, the outside: from, it might even be said, the perspective of the regionalist/outsider.

Amusements explores how T.V. and video culture trouble notions of perception, identity, and definitions of what is real; these concerns are conversant with Peter Narvaez's assertion that "for more than a century, rapidly developing technological media have been modifying the sensory experiences of the populations of Newfoundland and Labrador" (125). Communications technology does seem to have preoccupied Newfoundland writers: some of E.J. Pratt's work exemplifies this, as does the satirical depiction of T.V. in one of Ted Russell's Uncle Mose sketches, the poignant image of the woman watching a broken tv in an outport in Carmelita McGrath's poem "Mother's Lament," and the key roles of T.V. in Johnston's own *Divine Ryans* and *Bobby O'Malley*.

Narvaez cautions, however, against making the assumption that technological media simply sweeps into a regional culture, imposes its own "gestalt" on it, and decimates the uniquely indigenous aspects of a specific locale, including its folkloric tradition. More to the point, Narvaez argues, is to examine communications technology and regional culture as a site of interaction, a site which might be seen to approximate David Jordan's notion of region as a border-space. "In examining borders that define difference," Jordan writes,

> the regionalist author encounters confrontations not only along geographic borders that contain distinct local artefacts, but also along epistemological borders that define a particular sense of place, cultural borders that separate a distinct regional community from the larger society within which it exists, and aesthetic borders that define a distinct fictional world. On each of these levels, regional identity is constantly threatened by forces emanating from a larger world beyond its borders. The regionalist text is situated on these borders, and it is the regionalist's job to chronicle conflicts that shape a vital and evolving identity. (10)

Human Amusements constitutes such a site of interaction, chronicling, as it does, the confrontation between a small world—the Prendergast family and its three members, Peter, Audrey and Henry—and techno-culture's global agenda. This margin-centre conflict involves regionalist difference pitted against hegemonic, nationalized corporate centrality. The closer the Prendergasts move and are pulled towards the "centre," away from the original specificity of their St. Clair Avenue home with its basement rented out to marginalized figures, or "cellar dwellers" (4), the more endangered and fragile becomes their sense of themselves as a discrete entity, a family unit. Johnston's Prendergasts are forced, by tabloid reporters, gossip-mongers and hoards of fans, in effect, onto a kind of urban island where they are, paradoxically, quite marginalized yet seen everywhere through the medium of television.

What takes the place of difference and otherness in Johnston's postmodern T.V. world are media-produced, morality spectacles of Disney-like proportion. In *Amusements*, these spectacles, like the battle between Philo Farnsworth, the real and good inventor of T.V., and Victor Valensky, his sinister rival inventor, seem like clear-cut good versus evil conflicts, but they actually problematize identity. Henry Prendergast "becomes" Philo in a world where people seem to have trouble telling the difference between television and real life (256). Johnston would probably be skeptical of Frank Davey's contention, in *From There to Here*, that "the new media technology . . . radically enlarged the power of individual men" (13) and "diminished central authority and amplified individuals and counter-structures" (15). Johnston's novel acknowledges the power of media technology, but also its destructive potential to alienate and ultimately disempower individuals.

Yet Johnston avoids positioning his family—in other words, his "regional" constituent—as an entirely innocent, and thus, victimized, entity. If anything, *Amusements* illustrates how individuals participate in their own co-opting by media culture. He also shows how corporate production can also thwart individual artistic expression; this is exemplified through Peter, the angst-ridden writer/father whose literary career is almost entirely overshadowed by his wife's career in television. Audrey is completely seduced—at least during the novel's first section—by the fame T.V. success offers. As Henry narrates:

> My mother saw many parallels between Philo Farnsworth's life and her own. Philo's had been a rags-to-riches story, 'an Horatio Alger type of tale,' according to Everson. In fact, Philo had been an avid reader of Horatio Alger, deriving inspiration from the heroes of Alger's novels, self-made men who achieved success through self-reliance and hard work. When my mother, as part of her research for Philo Farnsworth, read one of Alger's works, she declared that her own life was an Horatio Alger-type of tale, though she was quick to point out that none of Alger's nineteenth-century protagonists had been women. (120)

Audrey's seduction by the Alger myth is delineated spatially, in terms of distancing, layers: readers read Henry watching Audrey reading Everson reading Farnsworth reading Alger in a kind of continual process of displacement. Indeed, the problem of displaced identity is chronic for Johnston's dislocated, if not utterly rootless, characters. The myths of identity filtered through literature (Alger) and into T.V. (through Farnsworth) almost destroy the Prendergasts as they struggle to maintain some kind of authentic bond between one another in the face of network politics and the tabloid discourse that threatens to envelop them.

Audrey, the mother, constantly endeavors to bestow some kind of collective identity on her family, but this maternally defined family/region is problematic; the Alger model is ill-fitting for several reasons. As Audrey herself recognizes, she is the wrong gender. Secondly, she does not realize until it is too late, or almost too late, that her identity as a "creator" is not really valued by the corporate networks; and thirdly, she is, more than she realizes, too idealistic and innocent for the corporate world. Henry refers to her at one point as his "lonely misfit saint mother" (274). Thus, Johnston's island of a family, reconstructed through the media as "the television Prendergasts," reflects a paradox of postmodern regionalism, being at once marginalized and isolated in the "cloistered life" (259) of their condominium tower, yet increasingly identified with media culture in their role as T.V. personalities.

In this paradoxical border space, which, following Jordan's analysis, could be said to approximate a regional space, discrete identity threatens to dissolve as Peter, Audrey, and Henry begin to appropriate the identities the media have constructed for them: Peter becomes the shadowy, mysterious absent father the tabloids make him out to be; Audrey becomes the manipulative, castrating mother "Miss Mary," an Orwellian "big mother" (29), and Henry becomes the rich, spoiled brat son who never seems to be able to get out from under his mother's thumb. Or so it would seem, until Johnston's novel concludes by suggesting that some kind of redemption, some reclaiming of small-world identity and solidarity might be possible.

Johnston's family, with its mother-breadwinner, reinforces the notion of T.V. as feminized space, given that, as Lynn Joyrich remarks, "television has been represented in both popular and critical discourses alike as a 'feminized' medium," "truly a 'family affair'" with its "affective economy" (28). T.V.'s central position within domestic space, Joyrich argues, has nationalist implications as well: "bringing its families into our living rooms and us into theirs, television asserts a national family unity even as its patterns of use within the home articulate relations of power, positioning the family unit within a wider social sphere" (28). Thus motherhood and nationhood would appear to be closely and uneasily intertwined, and part of what is "wrong with the picture" in *Amusements* seems to be the tyrannical dominance of both. That "something is wrong with the picture" in Johnston's urban, technological world is underscored by the inverted image on the Prendergasts' obsolete T.V. or "Gillingham," named after the tv repairman who installed the picture tube upside-down. The Gillingham figures centrally in the early part of *Amusements* as what Peter calls "an obscure rival of the television set," "an alternative technology" (14). The Gillingham, strongly humanized and eccentric, constitutes a critical "alternative" presence around the edges of Johnston's story, much like the numerous references—introduced mostly by Peter—to literature, another "alternative technology" in danger of being rendered obsolete by the video age.

Yet even those who champion the later, more sophisticated T.V. age, like Audrey, become a casualty of it. An important underlying irony in *Human Amusements* is that Audrey Prendergast's pre-eminence as a businesswoman is illusory; her authority erodes steadily throughout the novel in direct proportion to her success. "Miss Mary," Henry tells us, began to have a "haggard, weary look about her" (238). As the Philo Farnsworth fan club develops into a kind of groupie subculture, the Prendergasts' world becomes increasingly fragmented and irrational (256). Henry remarks:

> My mother was, to say the least, taken aback by how seriously some people took their television. She couldn't believe that all the good will she'd built up over the years could be undone in a matter of weeks. It was as if she had announced her plan to assassinate some beloved public figure. She hadn't known, she said, that there was so much bitterness, so much anger in the world, let alone that the mere possibility of the cancellation of a television program could bring it out. (256-7)

Clearly, Audrey has not grasped the contradictory nature of T.V. as a signifier, what Joyrich calls its "ambiguous position within the fluctuating arena of contemporary culture" (28). Contradictory in terms of gender, "feminized" T.V., Joyrich maintains, often blamed for disseminating puerile sentimentality, is also accused of "enormous phallic power . . . blamed for inciting the violence and unrest plaguing our culture" (28). "Such contradictions," she adds, are symptomatic of the shifting gender, familial, and consumer dynamics of ... American society," and "mirror similar appraisals of the postmodern condition" (28).

What is most instructive about Joyrich's analysis is the point of convergence it reveals between nationalism, postmodernism and electronic technology. In *Human Amusements*, the corporate-produced hysteria of the Philo Farnsworth fans who number in the thousands—satirically dubbed "Philosophers"—culminates in a surreal, apocalyptic spectacle which, significantly, I think, takes place in Maple Leaf Gardens. Johnston's decision to attach this national and nationalist signifier to a scene depicting the godlike appearance of Henry Prendergast dressed up as Philo Farnsworth, whose image is projected onto a Magni-vision screen (270), symbolizes the triumph of "the centre," which is at once the national and the technological, over the individual. With his Philo makeup on, Henry says he "looked like a kind of mask ... as though some quack mortician had done a rush job on [his] face ... like Philo come back from the dead" (270-1). "Everywhere I looked," he says, "I saw Philo, saw myself, writ large on the screen behind me, endlessly multiplied in front of me" (277): "screens within screens within screens, a line of ever-shrinking, ever-diminishing Philos stretching off into the centre as though into some limitless future. It was an often-used trick of the camera, but the crowd screamed its appreciation" (280).

During his appearance in front of the "video multitude" (279), Henry-Philo suddenly experiences an epiphany which fills him with "self-loathing" (277). It gradually dawns on him that his mother's T.V. career has driven a deep emotional wedge between himself and both his parents (275), that having become simply another image in a culture of constructed images, his ability to empathize with others has been seriously compromised, and that his demoralized father might never return home. Henry reflects:

> It seemed to me that my mother was to blame for everything, right from the start, that my father was right, that, by getting us involved in 'Rumpus Room,' she had ruined any chance we had for happiness, diverted us from our true course. I decided I would do what my father had done: I would leave her, get away from her for good, gain my independence, start to live my own life. ... If need be, I would

build myself some sort of estate, some secure and private place where
I would not be bothered. I assumed that I would have some sort of
family, that I would have companionship of some kind in this
cloistered life of mine. (259)

Henry's desire for a safe, "private" place, "some sort of family" and his wish to cloister himself on an island of his own making reflect the desires of the child-regionalist for a kind of primordial haven, to recall Mandel's identification—in Johnston's terms, a personal space free of video cameras and media-engendered, intrusive fans. A place where the original father and paternal order of things might be restored.

The prodigal father, Peter Prendergast, does come back home, in the novel's final scene. This return of the father points towards a reconciliation among the members of this dysfunctional T.V.-family; the novel ends just short of Peter's entrance, but Henry has seen his father approach the condominium tower. Paternal presence is imminent; thus the victory is Wayne Johnston's. His little island of a family has come close to disintegration, but the father, the family eccentric and wordsmith returning from the edges, re-introduces an oppositional, humanizing presence. Thus, the Prendergasts are saved by paternal authority—by the author, ultimately—at the last moment, from becoming victims of a chaotic, postmodern, virtual reality. In *Human Amusements*, a techno-apocalypse is supplanted by an essentially romantic longing for origin, for the "first place" and authorial (masculine) presence. The subliminal regionalism of *Human Amusements*, its core of sympathy for the misunderstood outsider, facilitates this return and re-instates the value of the margins.

Wayne Johnston's *Human Amusements* reveals how nationalized, corporate technology can upset the fragile chemistry of regions, both in the sense of distinct locales and the human "subcultures" identifiable as uniquely belonging to those locales. Further, Johnston's novel questions the status of literature itself within a media-dominated, postmodern society. Will the writer, surely the quintessential figure of difference and ex-centricity, simply turn into an anachronistic curiosity at best, or, at worst, disappear in the age of MTV? Will we be left only with nostalgic, backward glimpses at those unique, lost places that imprinted on each of us the stamp of individuality? In the twenty-first century, will longing become a prime expression, a key trope within "regional" literature? What new forms might "regional" literature take, if it continues to exist at all? These central questions posed by Wayne Johnston's T.V. novel resonate with a widespread unease, in contemporary society, over postmodern, electronic culture in an era of the worldwide web and an information highway which all too often bypasses the regions and homogenizes difference of various kinds.

RICHARD PICKARD *University of Alberta*

Magic Environmentalism
Writing/Logging (in) British Columbia

> To describe the beauties of this region will, on some future occasion, be a very grateful task to the pen of a skilled panegyrist. The serenity of the climate, the innumerable pleasing landscapes, and the abundant fertility that unassisted nature puts forth, requires only to be enriched by the industry of man with villages, mansions, cottages, and other buildings to render it the most lovely country that can be imagined. . . .
>
> (Captain George Vancouver)

THE INTERNATIONAL MEDIA simply does not tire of telling us that the world is metaphorically shrinking, that the grandest predictions of Marshall McLuhan are coming to pass in our time. The media's membership in multinational corporate society is of course the impulse toward this shrinking, so such enthusiasm is hardly surprising. What is surprising, however, is the extent to which self-styled global communicators must rely on specific location—in a word, on regionalism—to maintain their audiences. Print and screen ads place objects in context (sport utility vehicles in an African desert; cologne-wearing men in New York's Central Park); CNN interviews conducted in studios around the world occur before an easily identifiable backdrop of whatever city they happen to be in; American patriotism, including its manifestations in locations outside the United States, can scarcely have been more prevalent than it is in its new multinational, capitalist form.

Marshall McLuhan and Quentin Fiore in *War and Peace in the Global Village* summarize the basic theory behind the phrase "global village": "Today, electronics and automation make mandatory that everybody adjust to the vast global environment as if it were his little home town" (11). Franchise and monopoly capitalisms remove the notion of economic regionalism from international relations, as NAFTA and the EU testify. The question of how a Canadian logging community interacts with Fletcher Challenge, of how a village in India interacts with Union Carbide, cannot be asked; one must simply "adjust." Because global capitalism has resulted in cultural value being assigned to economic icons, and economic power being assimilated to cultural icons, the role of culture, and more specifically of art and literature, has become economic. Local theatre gives way to touring megaproductions; literary criticism gives way to cultural criticism; literary innovation gives way to franchise authors. McLuhan celebrates the role of the artist in the brave new world he imagines, but misses a step somehow: "He [the artist] glories in the invention of new identities, corporate and private, that for the political and educational establishments, as for domestic life, bring anarchy and despair" (12). The significance of "anarchy and despair" in "domestic life" falls by McLuhan's wayside, to be resumed by later writers.

Problematically, McLuhan seems to consider postmodernism as an entity without a driving force. Technology enables it, but offers no organizing principle: "Until we understand that the forms projected at us by our technology are greatly more informative than any verbal message they convey, we're going to go on being helpless illiterates in a world we made ourselves" (*Counter Blast* 122). In other words, the challenge posed by media and technology is a result of the technology itself; there is no consideration of control. Marxist theorist Fredric Jameson has different doubts on the subject of a controlling principle, and gives his 1991 book *Postmodernism* the subtitle *The Cultural Logic of Late Capitalism*:

> this whole global, yet American, postmodern culture is the internal and superstructural expression of a whole new wave of American military and economic domination throughout the world: in this sense, as throughout class history, the underside of culture is blood, torture, death, and terror. (5)

The thrust behind the multivalent cultural changes marshalled together as "postmodernism" derives from the economic machinery that drives the related phenomena of multinational and franchise capitalisms. McLuhan rarely discusses exactly what globalization means to the "little home town," but the ways in which the "little home town" adjusts to global capitalism are at the core of a particular strand of British Columbia regionalist fiction which addresses the role of logging, especially multinational corporate logging, in a specific and limited region.

The term "magic environmentalism" in the title of this paper is an attempt to borrow the claim for cultural specificity made of magic realist texts (particularly those from Latin and South America), while gesturing toward the centrality of environmental conflicts to representations of British Columbia. Conflicts, whether represented or not, are always already inherent within representations of the BC environment. In his discussion of Latin American magic realism, Jaime Mejía Duque has argued that "the actual relevance of a Latin American literature . . . has come to be incompatible with the evaluative schemes forged in the bourgeois European literary experience, the archetypal image until recently signifying universality" (12, my translation). He goes on to contend that "the real as an object of our writing is an irreducible ex-centricity/eccentricity [*excentricidad*], an objective unreality, for the egocentric metropolitan gaze" (81, my translation). Magic realism reflects local reality, for Mejía Duque as for Julio Calviño and others, but it is also a political response to the demands of writing one's own dialect(ic) version of the centre's language and literature. This kind of writing carries "within it, perhaps, a concept of resistance to the massive imperial centre and its totalizing systems" (Slemon 10).

As Stephen Slemon has noted, "In Latin America, the badge of magic realism has signified a kind of uniqueness or difference from mainstream culture . . . and this gives the concept the stamp of cultural authority if not theoretical soundness" (9). Theoretical soundness is clearly not a distinguishing feature of magic realism, as Amaryll Chanady has convincingly argued, but this in no way removes its cultural authority, particularly its authority to question established ways of ordering the world. In British Columbia today, environmental conflict is the largest single site of resistance to perceived mainstream culture. British Columbia writers, though not so visibly or forcefully oppressed by "metropolitan" control as Latin American writers, often see themselves writing from a similar location on the margins; the federal government, the United States, and multinational corporations act as the "totalizing systems" Slemon mentions here. Jack

Hodgins, for example, tells Geoff Hancock, "I suppose if there is a Canadian tradition, you probably mean the Upper Canadian tradition" (40), and specifically claims to "resist fictional forms which come from elsewhere" (48). (In the same interview, however, Hodgins also comments that "Man on Vancouver Island is not the victim of anybody except his own politicians and his real estate agent" [42].)

British Columbia stands as a frontier of sorts, dominated by tourism and resource-extraction industries. There is a paradox: what makes BC valued and unique is that which is being removed from it. On the one hand, tourists make BC a country foreign to itself; on the other, once the resource is fully extracted, the province's dubious celebrity is exhausted. Environmentalism has immense relevance to cultural questioning because the province's economic dependence on its forests is simultaneously a sign and a loss of identity. BC's identification with its forests—like that of any source of raw materials with (literally) its *raison d'être*—makes the questions raised by environmentalism particularly germane. Who owns a resource? who owns region? and what does the particularity of a region have to do with the extraction of resources? The fictions of Jack Hodgins, Peter Trower, and Brian Fawcett, in varying ways, address these questions. These three writers, all aware of McLuhanesque theories about globalism and of the monopoly capitalist economics controlling BC's resources, find highly individual methods to confront the destruction of region and the globalization of culture.

As Brian Fawcett writes in his poem "Poetic Words," "In an economic system grounded upon exploitation & energized by expansion/ the breakdown of common vocabulary is inevitable" (51). The attack on local community operates by provoking the breakdown of language as a signifying system. Whoever can hide this breakdown the longest can exploit it most fully. Accordingly, the traditional Marxist-style battle for the means of production has in BC become a battle for the means of description. Words have power, as George Orwell knew when he remarked in 1946 that "in our age there is no such thing as 'keeping out of politics'" (275). In 1990s BC there is no such thing as keeping out of environmentalism. The ongoing confrontation over land-use issues is an especially clear example of the terms "realism" and "reality" being hijacked by all sides. "Realistic" is used as a compliment by any group in referring to any description of the woods that supports that group's position. Natural description has been openly adopted as a political tool in this debate, and no one describing the woods can pretend any longer to neutrality. Even the provincial Ministry of Forests and Ministry of Environment, Lands and Parks are reinventing their perceived roles in the woods: "resource management" is becoming a forbidden expression, so both ministries are actively seeking new euphemisms.

If one group can gain control of language use, then it will control perceptions of the forest, and the battle for the forest as a resource base will be all but over—control the perception, control the reality. This has led to a proliferation of media conspiracy theories. For example, BC's newspaper of record, *The Vancouver Sun*, has had to defend itself from accusations by its own forestry reporter, Ben Parfitt, that it continually suppressed his stories. *The Sun* had contracted public relations specialists Burston-Marsteller to boost its circulation, but Burston-Marsteller had also been contracted by the Forest Alliance, a BC pro-logging coalition, to sell the idea of continued, unchanged logging. In other years, Burston-Marsteller has been hired

> by the Mexican government to help fast-track the North American Free Trade Agreement, by Hydro Quebec to peddle the James Bay II hydroelectric project, by Union Carbide after the company's Bhopal gas disaster in India, by Exxon after the Exxon Valdez oil spill, and by Argentina's military dictatorship in the seventies to lure foreign investment. (Goldberg 34)

Ken Rietz, an important figure in both Burston-Marsteller and the Forest Alliance, had been "a key figure in Richard Nixon's scandal-ridden 1972 re-election campaign" (Goldberg 37). Ben Parfitt, it is argued, never had a chance.

A second result of this pressure to control perception is that official government documents, which must at least attempt to seem neutral, must contend with a changing connotative vocabulary. Terms neither clearly euphemistic nor clearly pejorative are much in demand. Clearcutting has been called "even-age management"; hunting regulations speak of "harvested" animals. The currently preferred euphemism for cutting trees is somewhere between "harvesting" and "resource management," but the 1995 Kamloops regional Land and Resource Management Plan refers to areas open to logging as "enhanced resource development zones" (4).

Regionalism has become a flashpoint in the conflict. Environmentalist groups like Greenpeace condemn logging companies like Fletcher Challenge as multinationals, who, by reason of their transient status, have no abiding interest in any particular region, and the logging companies fight back by calling their harvesting strategy "community planning." BC pro-industry groups exploit the dominance of environmentalist attitudes in Vancouver and Victoria rather than in the rural areas most affected by job losses, as well as the truly multinational base of environmentalist groups Greenpeace and the Sierra Club. The question of definition becomes one of the right to define; control, both sides agree, should go to the side most deeply representative of the community. As a result, both try to make the other look like a monolithic, urban-based, faceless corporation; both claim to defend the local, the particular, the regional.

Language in the environmental debate goes toward justifying one group's dominance over the forest and over the other groups. Among all the competing systems of language, two in particular are available to those people writing or speaking on this subject: the local and the abstract. The local appears in phrases like "community planning," the abstract in "enhanced resource development zones." These systems apply not just to the primary competitors in the debate, but to all those writing about it. Hodgins describes a community's relationships in relentless detail to express its interconnectedness, Trower describes locale accurately in order to advocate change in logging practices, and Fawcett rejects local colour entirely and chooses to colonize the language of government publications for his own enunciation of positions much like Trower's. Trower and Fawcett especially seek to defend the regional particularity threatened by logging companies, but all three writers base their aesthetic practices in the celebration of region.

I first encountered Peter Trower as a logger and a poet in Tom Wayman's 1981 *Going for Coffee: An Anthology of Contemporary North American Working Poems*. Because my father is a millworker, my grandfather was a faller, and my uncle is a professional forester, Trower's poetry had very ready meaning for me; its coding, poised between celebration of the work and respect for the land, made his writing accessible to me because of my own knowledge of the kind of work he described.

What I enjoy about Trower's poetry is its refusal to separate the work from the woods, the men (and women) from the machinery from the trees. The conservationist 90s have not altered this focus, but they have drawn him into joining the fight against the old ways of logging that he participated in during his 22 years as a logger.[1] Trower's novel, *Grogan's Café*, about protagonist Terry Belshaw's first year as a logger, praises Terry by celebrating his sensitivity to logging's destructiveness. You as the reader are encouraged to recognize the limited perspective of the hero's brother when he says, "Logging's a messy business all right . . . no doubt about that. Tears hell out of the country. But the trees'll grow back before they run out of timber in this bloody province" (44). The irony is, of course, that by the time this book is written, forested land has been redefined as something other than unconverted cash; the province, in this sense, has now run out of timber. In *Grogan's Café*, logging can only be redeemed if it is performed with respect; Lasarek, a hooktender who rapes a faller's wife and dies when the faller drops a tree on him in revenge, logs as he treats people: "As though logging were some sort of personal vendetta, he went at it with a sadistic joy, glorying in the carnage and the violence" (98-99). Lasarek is a company dupe just as much as a self motivated malevolence; however much he enjoys the "carnage," he is still the worker preferred by the woods boss. Terry's basic goodness is even more self-motivated than Lasarek's evil, but he sees equally through the company rhetoric of replanting and through the mythic tales of an infinite resource base. He talks of "raw acres of devastation, the stark battlegrounds of the logging camps, great brown scars of slash where the forest had been stripped away like hide under a skinning knife" (43-44), and calls fallers "executioners of the timber" (51). After noting how at one location the loggers "continued to smash up the landscape," Terry complains that it was "like destroying a shrine. . . . Logging was a damn brutal business when you looked at it this way. It left nothing but ruin in its wake" (98). Terry owns the singular gift of being able to change perspective, to look at forestry "this way." This gift is a result of his place within the industry, but also of his native sensitivity.

Both Trower and his character are obsessed with accuracy in their descriptions of forests and the results of forestry. But the irony of one's expectations is that Terry clearly cannot maintain his position as both conscientious objector and forest industry wage-earner: the reader is convinced that Terry must choose one or the other. But he doesn't. He chooses no such thing. Just as Peter Trower did after his first year as a logger, Terry

Belshaw spends the next 21 years of his life cutting trees. *Grogan's Café* is specifically about logging and loggers, and is a celebration of a craft that Trower cannot, in these conservationist times, celebrate carelessly. Because of this need for caution, there is no conclusion as such to *Grogan's Café*, except for the narrator's realization that after working as a logger, "You're a logger now whether you think so or not" (227). The book's final paragraph, its coda, simply remarks that Terry's story continues for a period much longer than that covered by the novel. By avoiding conclusion and closure, Trower avoids the pressure of moral decision. His character (a thinly disguised autobiographical subject) works for 22 years in forestry, in spite of his objections to it. It is specifically the narrator's quasi-genetic ties to the forest industry that give him the authority to criticize it through his expressed attitudes, just as it is Trower's ability to describe the industry accurately that allows him to criticize it in realist, regionalist fiction.

This obsessiveness with specificity leads to fiction writers having to distinguish their writings very carefully from nonfiction. The fictional text's obligatory protestation not to represent objective reality is one site where this conflict between representation and reality can be overtly discussed, and Jack Hodgins confronts the need to separate fiction from reality in the legalistic disclaimers to both his first two novels. In his first novel, *The Invention of the World*, the lines are incorporated into the text of the novel, receiving a separate page immediately after the dedication and before the fictional preface:

> This is a work of fiction; its characters and situations are imaginary. Though there have been and still are several colonies of various types on Vancouver Island— some with colourful leaders and a few with histories of scandal—none of them has served as a model for the Revelations Colony of Truth. (vi)

Hodgins makes it very clear that he is aware of the historical fact of colonization on Canada's We(s)t Coast. Rather than ending with the bland first sentence, which contains all the disclaimer that the law of genre demands, he instead implies that his represented colonization, though factually different from "real" colonizations in the historical record, is close enough that it needs to be specifically distinguished from them; this is, of course, a ruse with which to defend his personal reconstruction of the record. Hodgins has said that he writes "Lies that tell the truth" (Hancock 62). The historical specificity of *The Invention of the World* is central to the novel, and first appears in this initial theft and recycling of the language of a historicality.

Hodgins places an even more comprehensive disclaimer on the copyright page of his second novel, *The Resurrection of Joseph Bourne*:

> This is a work of fiction. Though Port Annie shares some of its geography and a little of its history with actual towns in the northern region of Vancouver Island, it is a product of the imagination, and its inhabitants are not to be confused with actual persons, living or dead. Since there is sometimes a tendency to equate fictitious public figures with actual public figures, it is perhaps necessary to state that Jacob Weins, who shares some obvious surface characteristics with other Island mayors, grew naturally from the fictional soil of Port Annie and is not intended to represent anyone but himself. (iv)

Because Hodgins, like Trower, is so concerned with descriptive accuracy, he takes considerable pains to clarify the generic allegiances of his text. He considers himself a realist, in spite of convincing arguments by Cecelia Coulas Fink, Susan Beckmann and others that his fiction is less realist than magic realist: "What may appear like 'magic' realism to someone else is just 'pure' realism to me. I believe in my own fictions" (Hancock 57). Although critics such as Allen Pritchard have largely accepted Hodgins's claims, I would argue that the reality or realism in Hodgins's fiction is not for local colour, as Pritchard suggests, but to enable a regionally based criticism.

One vehicle for Hodgins's criticism in *The Invention of the World* is Maggie Kyle's use of maps. Maggie is the one character who best knows what Vancouver Island is about; excluding the nomadic Madmother Thomas, Maggie has lived in the most places on Vancouver Island, and she knows them all personally. She has pinned on her living-room wall a "row of pale brown nautical charts" and "[g]as-station maps of the island, a brilliant unnatural green." In addition,

> Four grey timber survey maps of the mountains told her just exactly how the crown land had been divided up among the logging companies and then divided once again into different lots and settings. Maggie kept track of all their progress, they needn't think that no one knew what they were up to. (44)

Not only does Maggie know the island from her life on it, but she keeps track of the changes that occur everywhere on it. Her desire is not to know or to learn the area represented, as it is for so many map-collectors, but to maintain the island through her continuing knowledge of it:

> She hated the maps, or what they showed her, and yet she could not have done without them. . . . The surveyors and the land-developers were there to create borders and to try to change the nature of the land, and there was something in her that found the business foul. (44-45)

The island is changing; its life is changing. Maggie Kyle is the character charged with defending her place, and so it is in this sense fitting that her story, *The Invention of the World*, ends with a Bakhtinian carnival of a wedding that consummates her integration into and influence over her community.

The Resurrection of Joseph Bourne also ends with a carnivalesque celebration, the last dance of the great Jenny Flambé, a touring stripper who has settled in tiny Port Annie. After the mountain slides down on top of the town, burying it under tons of mud, there is nothing to do but begin again, as one-industry towns do after natural disasters. The pulp mill will come back, or it won't; either way, the people of Port Annie will have their town waiting for its return, and Flaming Jenny dances the townspeople's energies back into them. Ironically, tragically, it is the pulp mill's taste for profit that destroys the town by logging the hillside above it:

> The Mill owners knew it was going to happen, those lousy money-grabbers. They were just looking for an excuse to close the Mill anyway, this was what they hoped would come along and solve all their problems for them. (249)

Gradually, the explanation becomes a conspiracy theory, moving from the mill to higher powers with less visible and therefore more threatening control over the future of the town:

> That damn government knew it was bound to happen sooner or later. They sent their inspectors up to look things over after the other slides, they could've done something to stop it then, but what did they care

about Port Annie? They knew the town had supported the
Opposition. (249)

Finally, the blame goes where it has been heading throughout the novel, as several foreshadowing descriptions of the logged hillside above the town have implied:

Those logging companies were the ones who'd started it. They should've refused to cut the timber off that hill, the dumbest thing anyone had ever heard of, not a brain in their heads. Some people would do anything for money, no matter how stupid. (249)

The final reason for the catastrophe, though, the one the reader is left with as definitive, is that the realtors planning a seaside resort escape in Port Annie would now be able to buy land more cheaply; Hodgins's comment to Hancock about Vancouver Island realtors, quoted above, seems relevant here. Logging's demonstrable impact on erosion and land-form stability is ignored, covered up by the conspiracy theories provoked by the sense of a community under siege; the logging company is staffed by the town, so the forces of evil must therefore come from elsewhere. Hodgins makes sure that money is at the root of the successive dominations of the town by the mill, the government, the logging companies, the realtors, just as Fredric Jameson would argue it would be. Money from outside sources, in the end, destroys the community of Port Annie.

Like Hodgins, Brian Fawcett also emphasizes community in his first two novels. Although Fawcett's textual strategies are in general very different from those of Hodgins, Fawcett includes similarly unconventional fictional disclaimers. The Grove Press hardcover edition of his 1986 novel, *Cambodia: A Book for People Who Find Television Too Slow*, includes the ironic disclaimer "All resemblance to real persons, living or dead, is purely coincidental, right?" (iv). In *Public Eye: An Investigation Into the Disappearance of the World*, in which Fawcett includes his challenge to fictionality in a larger attack on the modes of cultural transmission, he offers the disclaimer "Like the evening television news, this is a work of fiction. All resemblances to real persons and things, living or dead, is purely intentional—unless they find it objectionable, of course . . ." (v, ellipsis in original).

For Fawcett, the salvation of region in literature has become rather more difficult than simply describing it meticulously, which has been the time-honoured method for preserving BC as a region in literature. This is not just a reference to Peter Trower and Jack Hodgins; I think of poet Robert Swanson, painter and writer Emily Carr, and writers Ethel Wilson and Linda Svendsen, along with others too numerous to mention. The only defence against becoming a gas station for the information superhighway is to become a coherent region, which means coming to an understanding of what your own region means. But Fawcett has reversed the regionalist call to arms: in order to preserve local regions, local environments, local communities, he has chosen to abandon his own region and write within and about the encompassing world cyberculture he condemns.

Brian Fawcett is interested in community, which is less specific to geography and topography than either Trower's or Hodgins's concepts of region. In *Cambodia*, Fawcett repeatedly engages a massive, anonymous, deregionalizing power. "The Huxley Satellite Dish," for example, illustrates cultural anachronism,[2] which Jaime Mejía Duque sees as integral to the ideological structure of Latin American postcolonialism, as a naturalized phenomenon in British Columbia. Although in the town of Huxley's opinion, BC's anachronism has been seen through and defeated, its defeat has come at the cost of all local culture. The good people of Huxley have bought themselves a satellite dish, hooked it up to the community cable system, and moved to Detroit. Fawcett slips into metafiction to explain this:

> You may be wondering how hooking a satellite dish into a community cable system can land a small town in British Columbia in the middle of Detroit, Michigan. You probably suspect that I've made up the town of Huxley and its satellite dish to illustrate some silly idea I have about how horrible the modern world is, and why you shouldn't watch television. . . . Sorry to disappoint you. This is as real as the evening news. The only difference is that the definition here is going to be sharper. (129)

Fawcett's target is not "television news," nor television itself, but cultural colonialism as practised by television and other modes of self-transmitting "culture." The recent cultural history of Huxley has been that of a poor cousin to Vancouver, itself a poor cousin to Toronto. Huxley's response is to ally itself with Detroit and receive its TV on Detroit time, believing in this way that it can circumvent the anachronism that subordinates Vancouver to Toronto as well as obviate the town's "real" cultural poverty beside Vancouver. Unfortunately, this only makes colonization more explicit by denying the exigencies of location and by living with Detroit's time and standards; it fails to make Huxley exist as its own cultural reality.

The changes are first visible among the town's adolescents. Baseball (remember the popularity of W.P. Kinsella's baseball novels) and basketball (1995 saw the introduction of the Toronto Raptors and Vancouver Grizzlies to the NBA) become the town's primary sports; for the first time in recent memory, nobody signs up for the high school kayaking club; natives and whites stop talking to each other and begin to emulate Detroit's racial division into the gangland enmity of "spades" and "honkys" (129). Adults begin to do their shopping on long lunch hours, to go to bed earlier (since Detroit's primetime ends at 8:00 in Huxley), and to cease outdoor recreation. They are "living in the future" (131), and they take every chance they get to remind friends and family in Vancouver of Huxley's progressiveness. They watch even more television, because they recognize Vancouver's cultural inferiority in Huxley's earlier reception of the same TV shows.

A Vancouver reporter, Chuck Cambridge, hears of Huxley's dependence on Detroit TV and decides to do a story on it. Unexpected problems arise. The leader of a native gang refuses to talk to Chuck upon learning that he is from Vancouver, not from either Detroit or Dearborn: "Vancouver's noplace. Chieftains don't talk to cameras from Vancouver. Get out of my face, y'hear?" (137). When Chuck tries to explain the reasons for time-delayed broadcasting from the East (demonstrating his complicity with Western Canada's current situation of colonialism through cultural anachronism), Doris Klegg tells him, "It doesn't matter when things happen anyway. It's when people find out about them that counts. And we know about everything three hours before you do" (137-38). Jimmy Martin, an unemployed forest sector worker who watches twelve to fifteen hours of television every day, isn't too concerned about his unemployment, because he expects to find "something in the auto industry. You may not know about it, but things are looking up these days in the industry" (140). His phrase "the industry" is ominous, implying that he has no sense of any other reality beside Detroit's. The objections that the book would have its readers make are fairly obvious (Doris should realize that it's what actually happens that counts, not when it happens or when you hear about it;

Jimmy's belief in the auto industry as his employment saviour reveals that he cannot understand his own local economy; and so on), but Chuck Cambridge, representative of the TV empire, does not explicitly make those objections.

Chuck does briefly wonder why the national news programs are broadcast in British Columbia three hours after they are taped, making them always already out-dated, but he fails to speculate on the sociocultural meaning of anachronism. He could have been more specific in his wondering and recalled the usual anger in British Columbia on national election night at being informed as the live national news reports begin that before a single vote is counted in BC, Canada's ruling and opposition parties have already been decided, but he doesn't. Chuck is mildly satirized for not noticing this apparent irrelevance, but he is nevertheless correct to find Huxley's suburban relationship to Detroit worrisome. For Fawcett, simultaneity with a colonizing centre that destroys local culture — as Huxley's mythic "Detroit" does — is no solution to colonization.

For the residents of Huxley, whether they know it or not, Toronto and Detroit are simply alternate colonial centres against which towns like Huxley should be fighting. The battle, Fawcett fears, should have been joined long ago. "Universal Chicken," another story/chapter from *Cambodia*, opens its attack with a second-person description of an encounter with a huge gas station after a morning of freeway driving. Imagine that when you drive into this gas station, you suddenly aren't quite sure where you are, because you see absolutely nothing that you haven't seen at any number of other gas stations. The signs you've seen on the freeway today don't help, because they're signs that you've seen repeatedly over the last several days. This is the narrator's summary of your thoughts on the matter:

> The villain is wraparound North America. And you understand, with a helpless sensation, that it is closing in on you and on this small planet.
>
> Every day now it gets worse. More total. When you pull into a motel tonight, you will probably fall asleep watching the same television spectacles that merchandise millions of other people into temporary oblivion after a full day of being assaulted by the franchise products that have been assaulting you all morning. It's a subtle assault, of course. At least until you recognize that you're being colonized and controlled by it. (59)

Fawcett's particular regionalism in this story is an apocalyptic warning of a post-regional world, once total consumer colonization has been accomplished. Like the rest of *Cambodia*, as well as the later *Public Eye*, "Universal Chicken" is about the kind of human world that remains once "Planet of the Franchises" (*Cambodia* 58) takes over completely. The point is not specifically region, as it is for Hodgins and for Trower, but the dissolution of it; Fawcett writes not a celebration of local eccentricities and particularities, but an attack on the blandness that comes after the end of region. To refer back to Fawcett's poem "Poetic Words," "Those who will not join the struggle for control over the tools of meaning pass alms to the priests of capital who grow fat/ on our divine substance" (51). Individual regions must recognize their unique "divine substance," and must separate themselves from the shadowy "priests of capital." The "tools of meaning" are all a region has to work with.

Fawcett's second novel, *Public Eye*, takes place in barely individualized locations: a generic chain restaurant in a generic mall in Akron, Ohio, which he makes a generic town at the centre of wraparound North America; suburbs; a generic low-cost housing complex so unindividualized that even the residents get lost in it. The only story that mentions the environment as such takes place in the Sisk Valley, in "the Northwest" (9), but it makes reference to it only as a threatened space: "The countryside is pretty where it hasn't been logged off, the rivers are still reasonably unpolluted, and the air is clear and clean once you get a few miles beyond the pulp mill" (10).

As in *Cambodia*, Fawcett in *Public Eye* does not accept that a regionalist literature is available to him, even though his political program is to defend the right to region and to local community. The world has changed:

> The Global Village is turning out to be eminently urban in character, not sylvan. Because it is primarily an output system, it has imperialized its megalopolitan obsessions and its consumerist values into the hinterlands, making the entirety of North America an economic and cultural monoculture. The hinterlands have become impoverished suburbs of a limited number of megalopolitan output and profit collection centers. In North America that means New York and Los Angeles, and if Canada is lucky, Toronto. (194-195)

It is not that region and location are irrelevant, not to Fawcett and not to the Global Village, but that the whole notion of region has come under attack by language such as that which Fawcett adopts in his writings. The cyberculture constantly touted as just around the next corner of the Information Superhighway will occur in every person's living-room, or study, or kitchen, or bedroom. These places are all indoors; if there is no reason to go outside, region and location have lost meaning. There is no such thing as a village, because this is a world of "cities too large for place & names" (Fawcett, "Cottonwood" 17). Because the world has evolved beyond seeing relevance in "place & names," regionalist realism offers no defense of region.

After all this implied polemic about the need to defend region and particularity, some realities need to be faced about naive regionalist defenses. Disney is everywhere. Texts, especially with the increase in electronic media, cannot be limited to circulation within their home region. The environment exceeds all regional and national boundaries. Robert Kennedy Jr. was welcomed into the Clayoquot Sound conflict by the region's tribal elders, in spite of their continuing attack on the multinational character of the logging companies involved.

One of my favourite poems about the new economic internationalism is Tom Wayman's "Picketing Supermarkets," which purports to be a store manager's response to a protester's argument that a supermarket's international trade hurts the region in which the store is located:

>   all this food is grown in the store
>   . . . .
>   Cabbages, broccoli and tomatoes
>   are raised at night in the aisles.
>   . . . .
>   This chain of stores has no connection
>   with anyone growing food someplace else.
>   How could we have an effect on local farmers?
>   . . . .
>   And there are no Nicaraguan heroes
>   in any way connected with these bananas. (600)

Wayman, who has been living in British Columbia for many years, shares similarities with Brian Fawcett, most notably this animosity toward the destruction of region. Of course an importing store hurts local farmers; it is the need to hide this basic fact that has driven so many grocery monoliths to look local, to have catchy jingles about being in your neighbourhood, and to invoke images of the garden market as a way of cloaking their steel and stucco walls in rhetoric. As Jameson argues, the economic variation of postmodernism is all about cloaking, because it has to conceal itself; "the underside of [postmodern] culture is blood, torture, death, and terror" (5).

I'll quote Fawcett one last time, this time from a prolonged rant against academic literature: It's not that we in Canada are

> afraid to understand or criticize our political, social, and intellectual culture. The problem most of us have is that we can't recognize any specific culture among the Disney icons, the televised incitements to violence and conspicuous consumption, and the consumer franchises that bleed local economies and cultures of their vitality. ("Postmodern" 63)

In an essay on the possibility of television ever being educational, Fawcett remarks that "a cold-eyed scan of television viewer demographics testifies to the medium's actual mission: to reduce us to a Disneyfied lowest common social denominator, to sell us standardized merchandise and ideas, and to ship the profits to New York and Los Angeles" ("Interesting Times" 233). This notion of a centre to globalism is part of the key to Fawcett's deep difference from McLuhan. While Fawcett agrees with McLuhan that the basic form of technology threatens current (and current versions of utopian) cultural formations, he also remarks on the tremendous centralization of power in the global economy. Media technology, like franchise capitalism, leads not to greater local involvement but to greater corporate domination.

Postmodernism, in its techno-evil economic incarnation as the Global Village, threatens the whole idea of meaningful community as the/a focus of region(alism). Peter Trower, Jack Hodgins, and Brian Fawcett are justifiably nervous about being perceived as having any sort of allegiance with postmodernism, and therefore defend their home region from the threat of postmodernism's economic and political corollary, but all three have connections with its literary manifestation. What makes Fawcett unique among BC writers in his postmodern regionalism is that he argues in explicitly confrontational fiction the meaning of words like culture, and society, and region; neither Hodgins nor Trower does this, and I would argue that this is a direct result of their perceiving regionalism as realism. Realism is not enough, Fawcett protests; the idea of community is more important than geography, botany, or topography, so that is his emphasis. Postmodernism itself is not the evil, in spite of what so many defenders of region argue; the evil is the world of monopoly capitalism that signifies postmodernism for well-known theorists like Fredric Jameson and obscure fiction writers like Brian Fawcett.

Notes

1. The "old ways" are the hundred or so years between octogenarian active logger Merve Wilkinson's even older ways of horse-logging and selective harvesting of individual trees, and the new ways in the postconservationist future that the Clayoquot protesters imagine; Wilkinson was one of those arrested for protesting at Clayoquot Sound. For information about Wilkinson, see Iain Dawson Cuthbert's "The Man from Wildwood" in Howard Breen-Needham's *Witness to Wilderness*. For information about technological change in logging, see Don Malcolm's "Loggers: The Glory Days," 109-13; and Gary Snyder's "Ancient Forests of the Far West" in John Ellison's *Beloved of the Sky*. 137-61. A good history of logging around Prince George, Brian Fawcett's home town, is Ken Bernsohn's *Cutting Up the North*. An accessible but strongly pro-industry guide to forestry in BC is *The Working Forest of British Columbia*.

2. Cultural anachronism is the state of living permanently behind the times; Mejía Duque defines it as an inability to create any kind of local, regional structure, but to have to imitate that which is learned from somewhere else. In the case of Latin America, that means Spain; in the case of British Columbia, that means eastern Canada, the United States, and England.

JONATHAN HART   *University of Alberta*

Afterword

Sense of Place:
A Response to Regionalism

A PARADOX OFTEN INFORMS ART: if artists embrace the places they live, no matter how remote, they are more likely to speak to those who live in the political and economic centres. This is no easy task, for capitals often exercise great influence on the regions they control. Paris and London dominate France and Britain. Hollywood and New York exercise great influence in popular film and fashion. In great federal states, like Canada and the United States, there are several historical reasons for decentralization in culture. The American colonies involved a fracturing from the beginning. Spanish, French, Dutch and English colonies in North America, from Florida to Newfoundland, were precarious until the mid-seventeenth century. From the beginning, North America was multinational and multicultural. The Swedes, Basques, and Portuguese also tried to create settlements in North America, a land much vaster than Europe. The indigenous peoples spoke a wide array of languages and dialects and ranged from the Aztecs in Mexico, with their vast cities and temples, to the Cree, who hunted and wandered the Canadian Shield and Great Plains. The English colonies at Newfoundland, Jamestown, Bermuda and Plymouth did not develop major cities. Philadelphia, New York and Boston did become major centres, but always in relation to London, even after the independence of the United States. Quebec was the capital of French America, but New Orleans developed an independent culture, as Guadaloupe and Martinique did. St. Augustine in Florida was on the northern rim of a decentralized Spanish America, which answered politically to Madrid and economically to Seville. Mexico City and Havana were important centres in the northern possessions of Spanish America.

In the nineteenth century, as the American nations, outside Canada and the Caribbean, won independence, a friction still occurred among the French-, Spanish- and English-speaking Americas. The United States absorbed parts of Canada and Mexico. Canada and the United States expanded west and north, so that new frontiers were always altering the cultural as well as political and economic map of the continent. Like Proteus, the nations of North America were changing shape, sometimes willingly, sometimes not.[1] The Europeans in these territories had to wrestle with change, trying to come to terms with colonialism, conflict with the indigenous populations and new identities. The Natives fought for survival. As much as Paris and London still guided culture in Canada and the United States, and as much as New York came to dominate life in the United States and Montreal in Canada, there were also political capitals like Ottawa and Washington and frontier towns growing apace in the West and North. The early Spanish and English colonies had often been like separate provinces, although New France had been more centralized, and this spirit continued after the independence of the United States and Canada. They just could not be like Britain and France as much as they tried. Mark Twain's Connecticut Yankee could only visit King Arthur's court. Hawthorne's Puritan New England and Twain's Mississippi travelled to England and were themselves. The English had to discover Robert Frost for him to be discovered in New England. William Faulkner's Yoknapatawpha made a small area in the South a synecdoche for the world in the minds of readers in many countries. In the 1960s, when Canada was shrugging off its colonial cringe, Margaret Laurence's Manawaka appealed to readers beyond the national borders, whereas decades earlier Morley Callaghan had published stories with American settings for American readers and Canadian settings for Canadian readers, or sometimes used anonymous settings that could be on either side of Lake Ontario or Lake Erie.

Culture can be curiously decentralized. This is especially true of painters and sculptors, who need galleries but do not need the vast investments of theatre companies in large centres. North America was always multicultural and faced great changes in culture. Internet, hyperspace and electronic publication in this the most wired continent in the world are creating new virtual regions in a vast and decentralized republic of culture.² In Canada, whose political power is moderate, a great deal of energy is expended in the various regions creating, producing and distributing art.

That is not to play down the influence of governments, corporations and centres in the production of culture in North America, but to say that the regions and alternative art forms and modes of production are modifying that control. That is one reason that this joint publication of the University of Alberta Press and *Textual Studies in Canada* on regionalism is so timely. It grows out of what, to my knowledge, was one of the first international conferences on regionalism. It raises important issues about the nature of regionalism in the United States and Canada and other questions of the relation of women, the canon, cultural difference, and postmodernism to studies of regions.³

Although I have emphasized the positive aspects of regionalism, regionalism itself is neither bad nor good. It can be used for positive or negative ends. The regionalist enterprise, as Marjorie Pryse notes, is not necessarily a working against universalism and dominant ideological assumptions; it can reinscribe stereotypes about Natives, African-Americans and women. She suggests that resistant narratives by men and women from outside the dominant culture can provide alternatives to this stereotyping within traditional regionalist texts. In this way regionalism becomes contrapuntal, a means of reading against the grain of the hegemonic or dominant cultural text. Here it is important to avoid reaction and to find alternative routes between centre and margin. Perhaps every discourse inhabits a region or seeks a putative regional audience even when it is produced at the centre. This phenomenon occurs in advertising in early Calvin Klein ads or in Marlboro Country. A certain ambivalence or manipulation can accompany such images. They can be projections from the city, what might be called urban pastoral. The persuasion of rhetoric needs to be resisted but not in a reactive way. To see the world in our grain of sand is an exhilarating task. Possibly then the different "I's" can begin to communicate through difference.⁴ Minute particulars are worth close attention. They should expand our various understandings of actuality, of realism and reality, not in their traditional senses but with expanding eyes.⁵

Regionalism has an ideological dimension that can blind us to the politics of margins as much as of centres. It is possible that we all inhabit an eccentric geometry of being on the rim and in the middle at once, even if Copernicus was said to have demolished this ancient epicyclical astronomy. Our eccentricity might be ideological. Comparing mythologies is multidirectional. Like Pryse, Frank Davey thinks it important to consider regionalism in ideological terms, and he sees regions as social creations and as being more closely related to geography than nations are. Davey warns that regionalisms in Canada can become new dominants that should be viewed sceptically. A cult of regionalism, as I have implied, is another cult. A critical engagement with regionalism is more likely to observe its ambivalence and to find something positive there. It is not easy to create alternatives in a variety of places without reproducing dominant modes and styles of commodification.

The ethnology of the local suggests that there is a fascination for the exotic in regionalism as much as in travel literature or the promotional literature of colonization, which begins in earnest with Columbus. David Martin points out that during the 1870s and 1880s *The Atlantic Monthly* mixed local colour fiction with anthropological writing. Cultural knowledge is a central theme to these apparently disparate forms of writing. Such ethnographical interest can mean a possession of the exotic or regional other, or that otherness can become a critique of the dominant culture. In speaking about the way Tacitus used the Germans to criticize Rome, Peter Burke has called this self-critical writing of the other the "Germania syndrome."[6] Another country, culture or region can provide alternatives to how things are being done at home. The King of Brobdingnag is trenchant in his critique of European imperialism.

This book includes specific examples of regionalism from the West and from Newfoundland to balance more general discussions of American and Canadian regionalism. In examining the conflict between logging and environmentalism in British Columbia, Richard Pickard discusses the division between realism and postmodernism in representing region. Is the global village, which is driven by capitalism, the root of the problem in the homogenization and destruction of regions? Perhaps fiction can read against the grain of all the trees consumed in a kind of macabre parodic version that steals its title from Browning's *The Ring and the Book*. The books themselves consume the forests as the loggers and tourists do. Region becomes a literal commodification. W.M. Verhoeven examines the West of 'Woman' in a discussion of geofeminism in the works of Aritha Van Herk. Geography, for women in the West, becomes a form of destiny or identity.[7] One alternative is to create a hybrid discourse, to mix fiction and history, as a feminist move against the masculine myth of the West. Is this

West a putative space or is it made material in the friction between ideology and discourse? Perhaps in fiction, as Pickard and Verhoeven suggest, alternatives can be created. The difficulty is that even with possible worlds the conflict is often material and, if it does not become so, it engenders an illusion without a future. In her reassessment of prairie realism, Alison Calder makes an interesting plea for a criticism that does not help to underwrite exploitation of the Canadian West by turning its great plains into "a permanent Palliser's Triangle," whose harsh wasteland makes it a prime location for development without responsibility, a kind of emptying out of a land that is uninhabitable. In discussing the Newfoundland of Wayne Johnson's *Human Amusements*, Jeanette Lynes also raises the issue of technology gutting meaning in a region. In such a view the information highway circumvents the regions and leaves a hypothetical nostalgia for writers as eccentrics, individuals writing from real places, and not members of an imagined homogeneity of the web. Postmodernism has a universalism that is potentially dangerous in its flattening consumerism. The region in these Canadian particulars becomes a utopian space of past and future.

While using regionalism as a form of cultural critique, it is also good to be wary of it: nostalgia can be exclusive and utopias have a nasty habit of becoming dystopias. Nonetheless, literature is a form of dream, and for all that it matters, an ideal. An interplay of the possible world of literature and theory as alternatives, with the scepticism that theoretical and literary representations often include, might provide one possibility in claiming and reclaiming the region without choking on the land itself. If "we" write from here, we need to ask whether there is any here here. That is part of the paradox that makes the creation of here, the centre of creation even on the rim of the world. The writer and reader dispute their home, their relation, wherever they are.

Notes

1. An early study of regionalism in both countries is Roger Gibbins, *Regionalism: Territorial Politics in Canada and the United States*. For a more general view, see David M. Jordan, *New World Regionalism: Literature in the Americas* and Reginald Berry and James Acheson, eds. *Regionalism and National Identity*.

2. There are, of course, dangers in the media of destroying any sense of place. Once again, it is how we use the media or regionalism that determines how positive it is. See, for example, Joshua Meyrowitz, *No Sense of Place: The Impact of the Electronic Media on Social Behavior*.

3. See, for instance, Judith Fetterley and Marjorie Pryse, *American Women Regionalists*.

4. See Jonathan Hart and Richard Bauman's, "Introduction," *Explorations in Difference: Law Culture and Politics*.

5. For the relation of the real and the regional, see Eric J. Sundquist's "Realism and Regionalism." *Columbia Literary History of the United States*.

6. Peter Burke, *Montaigne*, 46.

7. See Emily Toth, ed. *Regionalism and the Female Imagination: A Collection of Essays*, Gillian Rose, *Feminism and Geography: The Limits of Geographical Knowledge*, and Carol Shields, *The Republic of Love* (1992). At a talk at Harvard (10 February 1997), Shields referred to the view in *The Republic of Love* that "Geography is destiny..." (78).

Bibliography

Amabile, George. "Clearing the Field: Some Notes on Recent Poetic Theory." *Trace: Prairie Writers on Writing.* Ed. Birk Sproxton. Winnipeg: Turnstone, 1986. 91-99.

Anderson, Benedict. *Imagined Communities: Reflections on the Origins and Spread of Nationalism.* London: Verso, 1983.

Baker, Carlos. "Delineation of Life and Character." *Literary History of the United States.* Ed. Robert E. Spiller, et al. NY: Macmillan, 1948. Vol. II. 843-861.

Beckmann, Susan. "Canadian Burlesque: Jack Hodgins' *The Invention of the World.*" *Essays on Canadian Writing* 20 (1980-81): 106-25.

Bernsohn, Ken. *Cutting Up the North: The History of the Forest Industry in the Northern Interior.* North Vancouver: Hancock House, 1981.

Berry, Reginald, and James Acheson, eds. *Regionalism and National Identity: Multi-disciplinary Essays on Canada, Australia, and New Zealand.* Christchurch, N.Z.: Association for Canadian Studies in Australia and New Zealand, 1984.

Breen-Needham, Howard, ed. *Witness to Wilderness: The Clayoquot Sound Anthology.* Vancouver: Arsenal Pulp Press, 1994.

Brodhead, Richard. *Cultures of Letters: Scenes of Reading and Writing in Nineteenth-Century America.* Chicago: U of Chicago P, 1993.

Brodie, Janine. *The Political Economy of Canadian Regionalism.* Toronto: Harcourt, Brace, Jovanovitch, 1990.

Bronfen, Elisabeth. *Over Her Dead Body: Death, Femininity and the Aesthetic.* Manchester: Manchester UP, 1992.

Brown, E. K. "The Problem of a Canadian Literature." 1943. *Responses and Evaluations: Essays on Canada.* Ed. David Staines. Toronto: McClelland, 1977. 1-21.

———. *On Canadian Poetry.* Toronto: Ryerson, 1943.

Buckler, Ernest. *The Mountain and the Valley.* 1952. Toronto: McClelland & Stewart, 1982.

Buckner, P.A., ed. *Teaching Maritime Studies.* Fredericton: Acadiensis, 1986.

Burke, Peter. *Montaigne.* Oxford: Oxford UP, 1981.

Butala, Sharon. *The Perfection of the Morning.* Toronto: HarperCollins, 1994.

Cable, George Washington. *The Grandissimes: A Story of Creole Life.* 1880. New York: Scribner's, 1888.

———. "'Tite Poulette." *Old Creole Days.* 1879. New American Library. New York: Signet, 1961. 155-176.

Calviño, Julio. *Historia, ideología y mito en la narrativa Hispanoamericana contemporánea.* Madrid: Editorial Ayuso, 1987.

Chanady, Amaryll. "The Origins and Development of Magic Realism in Latin American Fiction." *Magic Realism and Canadian Literature: Essays and Stories.* Ed. Peter Hinchcliffe and Ed Jewinski. Waterloo: U of Waterloo P, 1985. 49-60.

Cooley, Dennis, ed. *Inscriptions: A Prairie Poetry Anthology.* Winnipeg: Turnstone, 1992.

———. *The Vernacular Muse.* Winnipeg: Turnstone, 1987.

Craddock, Charles Egbert [Mary Noailles Murfree]. "The Star in the Valley." *In the Tennessee Mountains.* 1884. Boston: Houghton Mifflin, 1886. 120-154.

Crapanzano, Vincent. "Hermes' Dilemma: The Masking of Subversion in Ethnographic Description." *Writing Culture: The Poetics and Politics of Ethnography.* Ed. James Clifford and George E. Marcus. Berkeley: U of California P, 1986. 51-76.

Cuthbert, Iain Dawson. "The Man from Wildwood." *Witness to Wilderness: The Clayquot Sound Anthology.* Ed. Howard Breen-Needham. Vancouver Arsenal Pulp Press, 1994. 256-62.

Dangarembga, Tsitsi. *Nervous Conditions.* Seattle: Seal Press, 1988.

Davey, Frank. *From There to Here.* Erin: Porcepic, 1974.

———. *Reading Canadian Reading.* Winnipeg: Turnstone, 1988.

Davidson, Cathy N. "Geography as Psychology in the Writings of Margaret Laurence." *Regionalism and the Female Imagination: A Collection of Essays.* Ed. Emily Toth. New York: Human Sciences Press, 1985. 129-138.

Davies, Gwendolyn, ed. *Myth and Milieu: Atlantic Literature and Culture.* Fredericton: Acadiensis, 1993

De Lauretis, Teresa. *Technologies of Gender: Essays on Theory, Film and Fiction.* Bloomington: Indiana UP, 1987.

———. "Aesthetic Theory and Feminist Theory: Rethinking Women's Cinema." *Female Spectators: Looking at Film and Television.* Ed. E.D. Pribram. London: Verso, 1988.

Dick, Alex. "Who is Hudson Kopochus? Questions about History and Nostalgia in David Adams Richards' Lives of Short Duration." Unpublished essay.

Dickinson, Emily. "Tell all the Truth but tell it Slant—." *The Complete Poems of Emily Dickinson.* Ed. Thomas H. Johnson. Boston: Little Brown, 1955. 506.

Eastman, Mary. *Dahcotah, or, Life and Legends of the Sioux around Fort Snelling.* New York: J. Wiley, 1849.

Eggleston, Edward. *The Hoosier Schoolmaster: A Story of Backwoods Life in Indiana.* 1871. Library Edition. New York: Grosset and Dunlap, 1892.

Ellison, John, ed. *Beloved of the Sky: Essays and Photographs on Clearcutting.* Seattle: Broken Moon Press, 1993.

Entrikin, J. Nicholas. *The Betweenness of Place: Towards a Geography of Modernity.* Baltimore: Johns Hopkins, 1991.

Fannon, Frantz. *Black Skin, White Masks.* Trans. Charles Lam Markhamm. New York: Grove Press, 1967.

Fawcett, Brian. *Cambodia: A Book for People Who Find Television Too Slow.* New York: Grove Press, 1986.

———. "Cottonwood Canyon: A Speech Meant to be Given to the Prince George Chamber of Commerce." *Creatures of State.* Vancouver: Talonbooks, 1977. 7-18.

———. "Interesting Times." *Unusual Circumstances, Interesting Times, and Other Impolite Interventions.* Vancouver: New Star Books, 1991. 229-37.

———. "Poetic Words." *Creatures of State.* Vancouver: Talonbooks, 1977. 51.

———. "Postmodern Fusions, Confusions, and Hypermodernism." *Unusual Circumstances, Interesting Times, and Other Impolite Interventions.* Vancouver: New Star Books, 1991. 60-67.

———. *Public Eye: An Investigation into the Disappearance of the World.* Toronto: HarperPerennial—HarperCollins, 1990.

Felman, Shoshana. "Turning the Screw of Interpretation." *Literature and Psychoanalysis.* Ed. Shoshana Felman. Baltimore: Johns Hopkins UP, 1982. 94-207.

Fetterley, Judith and Marjorie Pryse. *American Women Regionalists.* New York: W.W. Norton, 1992.

Fink, Cecelia Coulas. "'If Words Won't Do, and Symbols Fail': Hodgins' Magic Reality." *Journal of Canadian Studies* 20 (1985): 118-31.

Fleming, Berkeley, ed. *Beyond Anger and Longing: Community and Development in Atlantic Canada.* Fredericton: Acadiensis, 1989.

Forbes, E.R. *Challenging the Regional Stereotype: Essays on the 20th-Century Maritimes.* Fredericton: Acadiensis, 1989.

Frye, Northrop. Conclusion. *The Literary History of Canada.* Ed. Carl F. Klinck, et al. Toronto: U of Toronto P, 1967. 821-49.

Gibbins, Roger. *Regionalism: Territorial Politics in Canada and the United States.* Toronto: Butterworths, 1982.

———. "Western Canada: 'The West Wants In.'" *Beyond Quebec.* Ed. Kenneth McRoberts. Montreal: McGill-Queen's UP, 1995. 45-60.

Goldberg, Kim. "Axed: How the Vancouver Sun Became a Black Hole for Environmental Reporting." *Witness to Wilderness: The Clayoquot Sound Anthology.* Ed. Howard Breen-Needham. Vancouver: Arsenal Pulp Press, 1994. 34-41.

Goldman, Marlene. "A Deleuzian Analysis of Aritha van Herk's No Fixed Address and Places Far From Ellemere." *Canadian Literature* 137 (Summer 1993): 21-38.

Grove, Frederick. *Settlers of the Marsh.* 1925. Toronto: McClelland & Stewart, 1966.

———. "Snow." *Canadian Short Stories.* Ed. Robert Weaver. Toronto: Oxford UP, 1968.

Hancock, Geoff. "An Interview with Jack Hodgins." *Canadian Fiction Magazine* 32-33 (1979-80): 33-63.

Harding, Sandra. *Whose Science? Whose Knowledge?* Ithaca, N.Y.: Cornell UP, 1991.

Harris, Joel Chandler. "Azalia." *Free Joe and Other Georgian Sketches.* New York: Collier & Son, 1887.

Harrison, Dick. *Unnamed Country: The Struggle for a Canadian Prairie Fiction.* Edmonton: U of Alberta P, 1977.

Hart, James D. "Regionalism." *The Oxford Companion to American Literature.* 5th Ed. Oxford: Oxford UP: 1983. 632.

Hart, Jonathan, and Richard Bauman. Introduction. *Explorations in Difference: Law, Culture and Politics.* Toronto: U of Toronto P, 1996. 3-22.

Haslam, Gerald. "Introduction: Western Writers and the National Fantasy." *Western Writing.* Ed. G. Haslam. Albuquerque: U of New Mexico P, 1974. 1-8.

Hodgins, Jack. *The Invention of the World.* 1977. Macmillan Paperbacks 16. Toronto: Macmillan, 1986.

———. *The Resurrection of Joseph Bourne.* Scarborough, Ont.: Signet-Macmillan, 1979.

Hutcheon, Linda. *The Canadian Postmodern: A Study of Contemporary English-Canadian Fiction.* Toronto: Oxford UP, 1988.

James, Henry. *The Portrait of a Lady.* London: J.M. Dent, 1995.

Jameson, Fredric. *Postmodernism, or, The Cultural Logic of Late Capitalism*. Durham, North Carolina: Duke UP, 1992.
Jewett, Sarah Orne. *Deephaven*. 1877. *Novels and Stories*. Ed. Michael Davitt Bell. New York: Library of America, 1994. 7-141.
———. *The Country of the Pointed Firs*. Boston, 1896.
———. "William's Wedding." *Novels and Stories*. 556-566.
Johnston, Wayne. *Human Amusements*. Toronto: McClelland & Stewart, 1994.
Jones, Suzi. "Regionalization: A Rhetorical Strategy." *Journal of the Folklore Institute*. 13:1 (1976).
Jordan, David M. *New World Regionalism: Literature in the Americas*. Toronto: U of Toronto P, 1994.
———, ed. *Regionalism Reconsidered: New Approaches to the Field*. New York: Garland, 1994.
Joyrich, Lynne. "Going Through the E/Motions: Gender, Postmodernism, and Affect in Television Studies." *Discourse* 14.1 (1991-92): 23-40.
Kamloops Land and Resource Management Plan, Approval in Principle. Victoria, B.C.: Province of British Columbia, 1995.
Kaplan, Amy. "Nation, Region, and Empire." *Columbia Literary History of the United States*. Ed. Emory Elliott, et al. New York: Columbia UP, 1988. 240-266.
Kowalewski, Michael. "Writing in Place: The New American Regionalism." *American Literary History* 6.1 (1994): 171-83.
Kreisel, Henry. "The Prairie: A State of Mind." *Transactions of the Royal Society of Canada*, 4th ser., VI (June 1968): 171-80.
Kroetsch, Robert, ed. *Sundogs: Stories from Saskatchewan*. Moose Jaw: Thunder Creek Publishing Co-operative, 1980.
———. "Fear of Women in Prairie Fiction: An Erotics of Space." *Crossing Frontiers: Papers in Canadian and American Western Literature*. Edmonton: U of Alberta P, 1979. Repr. in *The Lovely Treachery of Words: Essays Selected and New*. Toronto: Oxford, 1989. 73-83.
Lecker, Robert. *Making It Real*. Toronto: Anansi, 1994.
Lenoski, Daniel, ed. *A/long Prairie Lines: An Anthology of Long Prairie Poems*. Winnipeg: Turnstone, 1989.
Loriggio, Francesco. "Regionalism and Theory." *Regionalism Reconsidered: New Approaches to the Field*. Ed. David Jordan. New York: Garland, 1994. 3-28.
Lutz, H. "'Meat and Bones Don't Matter': Mythology in *The Tent Peg*." *Ariel: A Review of International English Literature* 20.2 (1989): 41-67.
Lutz H., and J. Hindersmann. "Uses of Mythology in Aritha Van Herk's *No Fixed Address*." *The International Fiction Review* 18.1 (1991): 15-20.
Malcolm, Don. "Loggers: The Glory Days." *Beloved of the Sky: Essays and Photographs on Clearcutting*. Ed. John Ellsion. Seattle: Broken Moon Press, 1993. 109-13.
Mandel, Eli. "Images of Prairie Man." *In A Region of the Mind: Interpreting the Western Canadian Plains*. Ed. Richard Allen. Regina: U of Saskatchewan P, 1973. 201-9.
Mark, Joan. *Four Anthropologists: An American Science in its Early Years*. New York: Science History Publications, 1980.
McCourt, Edward. *The Canadian West in Fiction*. 1949. Rev. ed. Toronto: Ryerson, 1970.
McKay, Ian, and Scott Milson, eds. *Toward a New Maritimes: A Selection from Ten Years of New Maritimes*. Charlottetown: Ragweed, 1992.

McLuhan, Marshall. *Counter Blast*. Toronto: McClelland and Stewart, 1969.

———, and Quentin Fiore. *War and Peace in the Global Village: An Inventory of Some of the Current Spastic Situations that Could be Eliminated by More Feedforward*. New York: McGraw-Hill, 1968.

Mejía Duque, Jaime. *Narrativa y neocolonialismo en América Latina*. Medellín, Colombia: La Oveja Negra, 1972.

Melnyk, George. *Beyond Alienation: Political Essays on the West*. Calgary: Detselig, 1993.

Meyrowitz, Joshua. *No Sense of Place: The Impact of Elecronic Media on Social Behavior*. New York: Oxford UP, 1985.

Mitchell, W.O. *Who Has Seen the Wind*. 1947. Toronto: Macmillan, 1982.

Narvaez, Peter. "The Folklore of 'Old Foolishness': Newfoundland's Media Legends." *Canadian Literature* 108 (1986): 125-43.

Orwell, George. "Politics and the English Language." *The Essay, Old and New*. Ed. Edward P.J. Corbett and Sheryl L. Finkle. Englewood Cliffs, New Jersey: Blair-Prentice Hall, 1993.

Ostenso, Martha. *Wild Geese*. 1925. Toronto: McClelland & Stewart, 1990.

Parr, Joan, ed. *Manitoba Stories*. Winnipeg: Queenston House, 1981.

Porter, Bruce. Interview with Wayne Johnston. *Tickle Ace* 27 (1994): 12-29.

Postman, Neil. *Amusing Ourselves to Death: Public Discourse in the Age of Show Business*. New York: Penguin, 1985.

Potyondi, Barry. *In Palliser's Triangle: Living in the Grasslands 1850-1930*. Saskatoon: Purich, 1995.

Powell, John Wesley. *Introduction to the Study of Indian Languages*. 2nd ed. Washington: Government Printing Office, 1880.

Pratt, E. J. *Collected Poems*, Ed. Northrop Frye. 2nd ed. Toronto: U of Toronto P, 1958.

Pritchard, Allan. "Jack Hodgins's Island: A Big Enough Country." *University of Toronto Quarterly* 55 (1985): 21-44.

Pryse, Marjorie. "Reading Regionalism: The 'Difference' It Makes." *Regionalism Reconsidered: New Approaches to the Field*. Ed. David Jordan. New York: Garland, 1994. 47 64.

Quantic, Diane Dufva. "The Unifying Thread: Connecting Place and Language in Great Plains Literature." *American Studies* 32.1 (1991): 67-83.

Ricou, Laurie. Epilogue. *Vertical Man, Horizontal World: Man and Landscape in Canadian Prairie Fiction*. Vancouver: U of British Columbia P, 1973. Rpt. in *Essays on Saskatchewan Writing*. Ed. E.F. Dyck. Regina: Saskatchewan Writers Guild, 1986. 75-78.

———. *Vertical Man, Horizontal World: Man and Landscape in Canadian Prairie Fiction*. Vancouver: U of British Columbia P, 1973.

Robson, Peter A. *The Working Forest of British Columbia*. Madeira Park, BC: Harbour Publishing for I.K. Barber, RPF [Registered Professional Forester], 1996.

Rose, Gillian. *Feminism and Geography: The Limits of Geographical Knowledge*. Cambridge: Polity Press, 1993.

Ross, Sinclair. *As For Me and My House*. 1941. Toronto: McClelland & Stewart, 1985.

———. "The Painted Door." *The Lamp at Noon and Other Stories*. 1968. Toronto: McClelland & Stewart, 1991. 93-112.

Said, Edward W. *Culture and Imperialism*. New York: Vintage, 1993.

———. *Orientalism*. New York: Vintage, 1979.

Sangren, P. Steven. "Rhetoric and the Authority of Ethnography: 'Postmodernism' and the Social Reproduction of Texts." *Current Anthropology* 29.3 (June 1988): 405-424.

Shields, Carol. *The Republic of Love*. Toronto: Vintage Books, 1992.

———. "A View from the Edge of the Edge: A Look at Canadian Literature and How it is Perceived." Canada Seminar, Centre for International Studies. Harvard, 10 Feb., 1997

Shields, Rob. *Places on the Margin: Alternative Geographies of Modernity*. London and New York: Routledge, 1991.

Simpson, Claude M. *The Local Colorists: American Short Stories, 1857-1900* . New York: Harper, 1960.

Slemon, Stephen. "Magic Realism as Post-Colonial Discourse." *Canadian Literature* 116 (1988): 9-24.

Smith, Dorothy. *The Everyday World as Problematic*. Boston: Northeastern UP, 1987.

Snyder, Gary. "Ancient Forests of the Far West." *Beloved of the Sky: Essays and Photographs on Clearcutting*. Ed. John Ellison. Seattle: Broken Moon Press, 1993. 137-61.

Sproxton, Birk, ed. *Trace: Prairie Writers on Writing*. Winnipeg: Turnstone, 1986.

Stead, Robert. *Grain*. 1926. Toronto: McClelland & Stewart, 1993.

Steiner, Michael, and Clarence Mondale. *Region and Regionalism in the United States: A Source Book for the Humanities and Social Sciences*. New York: Garland, 1988.

Stenson, Fred, ed. *Alberta Bound*. Edmonton: NeWest, 1986.

Sundquist, Eric J. "Realism and Regionalism." *Columbia Literary History of the United States*. Ed. Emory Elliott, et al. New York: Columbia UP, 1988. 501-24.

Tefs, Wayne, ed., *Made in Manitoba*. Winnipeg: Turnstone, 1990.

Thacker, Robert. *The Great Prairie Fact and Literary Imagination*. Albuquerque: U of New Mexico P, 1989.

Toth, Emily, ed. *Regionalism and the Female Imagination: A Collection of Essays*. New York: Human Sciences Press, 1985.

Trower, Peter. *Grogan's Café: A Novel of the B.C. Woods*. Madeira Park, B.C.: Harbour Publishing, 1993.

———. "Overhead Crane," "Industrial Poem," "Early Shift," "Booby Trap," "The Beacons of the Bad Days." *Going for Coffee: An Anthology of Contemporary North American Working Poems*. Ed. Tom Wayman. Madeira Park, B.C.: Harbour Publishing, 1981.

Ursell, Geoffrey, ed. *Saskatchewan Gold*. Moose Jaw: Coteau, 1982.

Van Herk, Aritha. *A Frozen Tongue*. Sydney: Australia; Mundelstrup, Denmark; Coventry, United Kingdom: Dangaroo Press, 1992.

———. "Appropriations, the Salvation Army, and a Wager." *In Visible Ink: (Crypto-frictions)*. Edmonton: NeWest, 1991. 85-98.

———. *In Visible Ink (Crypto-Frictions)*. Edmonton: NeWest Press, 1991.

———. Interview. By Dorothy Jones. *SPAN* 25 (October 1987): 1-15.

———. *Judith*. 1978. rpt. Toronto: McClelland and Stewart, 1991.

———. *No Fixed Address*. Toronto: McClelland and Stewart, 1986.

———. *Places Far From Ellesmere*. Red Deer, Alberta: Red Deer College Press, 1990.

———. *The Tent Peg*. McClelland and Stewart, 1981.

Van Herk, Aritha, Leah Flater and Rudy Wiebe, eds. *West of Fiction*. Edmonton: NeWest Press, 1983.

Vancouver, Captain George. *Skookum Wawa: Writings of the Canadian Northwest*. Ed. Gary Geddes. Toronto: Oxford University Press, 1975. 65.

Warren, Robert Penn. "Not Local Color." *The Virginia Quarterly Review* 1 (1932): 153-60.

Wayman, Tom, ed. *Going for Coffee: An Anthology of Contemporary North American Working Poems*. Madeira Park, B.C.: Harbour Publishing, 1981.

———. "Picketing Supermarkets." *The Norton Introduction to English Literature*. Fourth edition. Ed. Carl E. Bain, et al. New York: W.W. Norton, 1986. 600.

Weimer, Joan Myers. "Women Artists as Exiles in the Fiction of Constance Fenimore Woolson." *Legacy* 3:2 (Fall 1986): 3-15.

Williams, Raymond. *The Country and the City*. New York: Oxford UP, 1973.

———. *Keywords: A Vocabulary of Culture and Society*. 1976. Rev. ed. New York: Oxford UP, 1983.

Wood, Ann Douglas. "The Literature of Impoverishment: The Women Local Colorists in America 1865-1914." *Women's Studies* Vol. 1 (1972): 3-45.

Woolson, Constance Fenimore. "In the Cotton Country." *Rodman the Keeper: Southern Sketches*. 1880. New York: Garrett Press, 1969. 178-196.

Index

Alger, Horatio, 87, 89–90
Amabile, George, 1
American expansionism, 87
Anglo-Quebec regionalism, 6–7
Atlantic regionalism, 14
Atlantic writing, 81
Austin, Mary, 32, 34, 38
authenticity, 57

Baker, Carlos, 44
Bakhtin, Mikhail, 104
Barnuow, Erik, 87
Baudrillard, Jean, 82
Beckman, Susan, 103
Bernsohn, Ken, 112n
Birney, Earle, 6
Bisoondath, Neil, 6
Blake, William, 78
Blaser, Robin, 6
Boas, Frank, 42
Bowering, George, 6, 81
Breen-Needham, Howard, 112n
British Columbia writing, 97–112
Brodhead, Richard, 42
Brodie, Janine, 2
Bronfen, Elisabeth, 80
Brown, E.K., 52–53, 56
Buckner, P.A., 9
Burston, Marsteller, 99

Cable, George Washington, 42–43, 46, 52–54, 55n
Calvino, Julio, 97
Canada Council, 13
canonicity, 5–6, 13, 115
capitalism, 12–13, 16, 87, 95–98, 110–112
carnival, 104
Carr, Emily, 106
Cary, Alice, 38
centre/region correspondence, 54, 56, 113. *See also* region as microcosm
Chanady, Amaryll, 97
Chesnutt, Charles Waddell, 32–34, 56n
Chopin, Kate, 43, 55n, 56n
Clemens, Samuel, 32
colonial centres, 113–114
colonialism, 1, 7, 11, 13, 102, 107–108, 113
and identity, 114
commodification, 5–6, 12–15, 98
Cooke, Rose Terry, 43
Cooley, Dennis, 11
Cooper, James Fenimore, 32
Craddock, Charles Egbert, 43–44, 51
Crapanzano, Vincent, 55
Creighton, Helen, 10
cult of regionalism, 116
cultural
anachronism, 106 (defined, 112, fn2),
codes, 63
colonialism, 106
globalization, 98

127

culture
    and decentralization, 114–115
    production of, 115
Curnoe, Greg, 15–16
Currie, Sheldon, 81
Cushing, Frank, 42–43
Cuthbert, Iain Dawson, 112n
cyberculture, 106, 110

Dangarembga, Tsitsi, 33
Davey, Frank, 89
Davidson, Cathy N., 61
Davies, Gwen, 10
Day, Frank Parker, 10
de Lauretis, Teresa, 61, 78, 79, 80
deconstruction, 76
Deleuze, Gilles and Felix Guattari, 3
determinism,
    geographic, 56
    environmental, 56–57
Dick, Alex, 9–10
Dickinson, Emily, 33
Dilthey, J., 45
documentary, 52, 56, 59
Du Bois, W.E.B., 29
Dunbar-Nelson, Alice, 34, 56n
Duque, Jaime Mejia, 97, 106

Eastman, Mary, 42
economic regionalism, 96, 113
Eggleston, Edward, 55n
Ellison, John, 112n
environmental issues, 97–99, 101–102, 105, 110. *See also* magic environmentalism
essentialism, 59
European Union, 96
Everson, George, 87

family, 85, 89–93
Fanon, Frantz, 11–12
Fawcett, Brian, 98, 100, 105–106, 109–112
Felman, Shoshana, 39

female identity, 61, 65, 74
female imagination, 61
feminism. *See* cultural feminism, geofeminism, prairie feminism
feminist standpoint theory, 29–31, 36, 37
Fetterley, Judith, 32, 38
Fink, Cecelia Coulas, 103
Fiore, Quentin, 96
Flater, Leah, 64
Fleming, Berkeley, 9
Fletcher, Alice, 42–43
Forbes, E.R., 9
Freeman, Mary Wilkins, 30, 42
Frye, Northrop, 4, 52

Garland, Hamlin, 42, 56n
gender roles, 86–87, 90–91
geofeminism, (defined) 62, 71, 77, 78
geografictione, 65, 77
geographic determinism, 2, 5, 56
Gibbins, Roger, 1–2, 7–8, 10
Gilbert, Gerry, 6
global village, 96, 109, 110–111
globalism, 1, 12, 14–16, 82–83, 86, 95–98, 109, 111
Goldman, Marlene, 73, 77
Greenpeace, 100
Grove, Frederick Philip, 51, 55, 59

Hancock, Geoff, 98
Harding, Sandra, 29–31, 35
Harris, George Washington, 32
Harris, Joel Chandler, 42–43, 47, 52
Harrison, Dick, 51, 57–59
Hart, James D., 41, 55n
Harte, Bret, 43
Haslam, Gerald, 57, 60
historical specificity, 103, 58
Hodgins, Jack, 6, 98, 100, 102–106, 109, 111–112
homogeneity, 83–84, 94, 108–109, 111
Howells, William Dean, 32
Hutcheon, Linda, 87

128 *Index*

indiginous peoples, and language, 113

Jackson, Helen Hunt, 56n
James, Henry, 26–28
Jameson, Frederick, 82, 96, 105, 111–112
Janes, Percy, 81
Jeffers, Robinson, 29
Jewett, Sarah Orne, 26, 28, 38, 42–43, 45–48, 53, 56n
Johnston, Wayne, 82–94
Jones, Suzi, 28
Jordan, David, 41, 59, 88
Joyrich, Lynne, 82, 90–92

Kaplan, Amy, 50, 55n
Keith, W.J., 5
Kerouac, Jack, 71
King, Clarence, 42
Kinsella, W.P., 107
Klein, Melanie, 36–37
Kreisel, Henry, 4
Kroetsch, Robert, 4, 10, 54, 57, 59, 81

Latin American writing, 97
Laurence, Margaret, 12, 61
Lawrence, D.H., 66–67
Lecker, Robert, 13
Leith, Linda, 6
Lenoski, Daniel, 11
literary canon, 25
literary studies, 1
local colour, 26–27, 42, 54, 61
local culture, 106, 108–109, 111
location (politics of), 77
logging, 97–99, 101–102, 104–105
Loriggio, Francesco, 28, 56
Lutz, Hartmut, 69, 71, 80
Lyotard, Jean-Francois, 83

MacLeish, Archibald, 60
MacLeod, Alistair, 81

magic environmentalism, 97. *See also* environmentalism
magic realism, 54, 97, 103. *See also* realism, prairie realism
Mahler, Margaret, 36
Malcolm, Don, 112n
male chauvinism, 69
Mandel, Eli, 84, 93
maps, 103–104
marginality, 89
Maritime regionalism, 8–9
Marlatt, Daphne, 6
masculinist discourse, 64–65, 78, 79
McCourt, Edward, 52, 56
McGrath, Carmelita, 88
McKinnon, Barry, 6
McLuhan, Marshall, 95–96, 111
media technology, 82–83, 85–94, 96, 106, 110–111
media, 95
Mejia Duque, Jaime, 97, 106, 112n
Melnyk, George, 12
Meyrowitz, Joshua, 82–86
Miller, Arthur, 71
mise–en–abyme, 77
Mitchell, W.O., 12, 58
multiculturalism, 95, 114
Murfee, Mary Noialles, 38

Narvaez, Peter, 87–88
nation-state, 1, 3–5, 7, 13, 91
  culture, 5, 92
  economics, 5
  history, 11
  politics, 5, 15
national myth, 63
Newfoundland literature, 83
Newlove, John, 12
Nietzsche, 78
North American Free Trade Agreement (NAFTA), 96
Northern regionalism, 7
nostalgia, 54, 85
novel, 81

Index 129

Ontario regionalism, 6
Orwell, George, 87, 98
Ostenso, Margaret, 52

Palliser's Triangle, 60
paradoxical space, 78
Parfitt, Gen, 99
parody, 87
Parr, Joan, 10
patriarchy, 65
Perry, Bliss, 34
political
 centres, 113
 feminism, 61
Porter, Bruce, 83
postcolonialism, 106
Postman, Neil, 82
postmodernism, 54, 81–82, 84, 86–87, 89, 92–93, 96–97, 106, 108, 111–112, 115
postregional culture, 109
poststructuralism, 62, 76
Powell, John Wesley, 55n
prairie
 fiction, 51, 58
 feminism, 63
 landscape, 58–59
 realism, 51–54, 56–60. *See also* realism, magic realism
 regionalism, 4, 6, 8, 10, 13–14
 writing, 12
Pratt, E.J., 5, 13, 86, 88
Pritchard, Allen, 103
Progressive Party, 8
Pryse, Marjorie, 55n, 56n

realism, 63, 102–103, 112
referentiality, 52
Reform Party, 8
region as microcosm, 56–57. *See also* centre/region correspondence
region, etymology, 28

regional
 anthologies, 1, 10–11
 change, 55
 literature, 52–53, 84, 93, 109
regionalism, 25, 41, 52–54, 60,
 aesthetic of, 32
 cult of, 115
 as critical term, 1, 3, 16–17
 as critique, 28
 defining, 2
 postmodern, 90, 112
 social construction of, 2
 subliminal, 84, 93
 West Coast, 6, 8, 14
regionalism and,
 anti-centrism, 4, 7, 11, 97
 community, 100, 104, 106, 110, 112
 cultural pluralism, 41
 culture, 4, 88
 difference, 3–4, 8–9, 12, 16, 84, 89
 discourse, 4, 7
 economics, 96
 environmental issues, 100
 geography, 2–4
 ideology, 1, 3, 5–6, 12, 17
 indentity affirmation, 15, 83, 90
 indigeneity, 11–12,
 political boundaries, 7–8
 political movements, 8
 populism, 5
 publishing, 14
 race, 34
 realism, 2, 102–103, 105, 110, 112
 resistance, 16–17, 109
 sectionalism, 15
regionality, 16, 85
representation, 62
Richards, David Adams, 5, 81
Richler, Mordecai, 6
Ricou, Laurence, 58–59
Rietz, Ken, 99
Rose, Gillian, 78
Ross, Sinclair, 13, 51, 55, 58
Russell, Ted, 88

Said, Edward, 25, 54
Sangren, P. Steven, 55
Scott, Gail, 6
sense of place, 82, 84–85, 88, 93
Shields, Carol, 61
Simpson, Claude, 48
Slemon, Stephen, 97
Smith, Dorothy, 30
Smith, Ray, 81
Snyder, Gary, 112n
spatial boundaries, 83
Sproxton, Birk, 11
Stead, Robert, 52
Stenson, Fred, 10
Sundquist, Eric J., 55n
Svendsen, Linda, 106
Swanson, Robert, 106

Tefs, Wayne, 10, 14
television, 82, 84–91, 93–94, 107–108, 110
territorialization, 3, 10
Thacker, Robert, 57, 59
Thaxter, Celia, 32
Thomas, Audrey, 6
Tolstoy, Leo, 74–75
Tourgee, Albion, 32
tragic vision, 51
Trower, Peter, 6, 98, 100–103, 106, 109, 111–112
Tylor, E.B., 43

Udelson, Joseph, 87
universality, 53–55
urban prairie, 54
Ursell, Geoffrey, 10

Vaccavari, Peter, 32
Van Herk, Aritha, 61–80
    and feminist agenda, 68, 76
Vancouver, Captain George, 95

Warren, Robert Penn, 55n
Watson, Sheila, 81
Wayman, Tom, 100, 110
Webb, Phyllis, 6
Weimer, Joan Myers, 50
West Coast regionalism, 6, 8, 14
Western Canada Concept Party, 8
Western regionalism, 10
White, Howard, 6
Wiebe, Rudy, 12, 64, 70
Wilkinson, Merve, 112n
Wilson, Ethel, 6, 106
Winnicott, D.W., 36, 37
Wood, Ann Douglas, 50
Woolson, Constance Fenimore, 42, 49, 51

Zitkala-Sä, 38

Other Titles in the Textual Studies in Canada Series

- **Textual Studies in Canada**
  Eds. Henry Hubert and W.F. Garrett-Petts
- **Authority: Begged, Borrowed, or Stolen?**
  Eds. W.F. Garrett-Petts, Henry Hubert, and James A. Reither
- **Reading and Writing Literary Histories**
  Eds. W.F. Garrett-Petts and Henry Hubert
- **Genre, Intextuality, Collaboration, and Other Struggles**
  Eds. James A. Reither and Douglas Vipond
- **The Aux Canadas Issue: Reading, Writing, and Translation**
  Ed. Robert K. Martin
- **The Conference Issue**
  Ed. Katherine Sutherland
- **Writings, Genders, Cultures**
  Eds. Ann Beer, Fran Davis, Claudia Mitchell, Anthony Paré, Cathy Paul, and Arlene Steiger
- **Politics, Pedagogy, and Masculinities**
  Eds. Daniel Coleman, Chris Bullock, Glenn Burger, and Andrew McTavish